A Time
to Break
Silence

OTHER BOOKS IN
THE KING LEGACY SERIES

"All Labor Has Dignity"

A Gift of Love

"In a Single Garment of Destiny"

Stride Toward Freedom:
The Montgomery Story

"Thou, Dear God":
Prayers That Open Hearts and Spirits

The Trumpet of Conscience

Where Do We Go from Here:
Chaos or Community?

Why We Can't Wait

Dr. Martin Luther King, Jr., is shown delivering the commencement address at Tuskegee Institute, Tuskegee, Alabama, May 31, 1965. (AP Photo/Horace Cort)

A Time to Break Silence

THE ESSENTIAL WORKS OF

MARTIN LUTHER KING, JR.,

FOR STUDENTS

MARTIN LUTHER KING, JR.

INTRODUCTION BY WALTER DEAN MYERS

BEACON PRESS

Boston

BEACON PRESS
25 Beacon Street
Boston, Massachusetts 02108–2892

Beacon Press books are published under the auspices of the
Unitarian Universalist Association of Congregations.

Beacon Press gratefully acknowledges the
Unitarian Universalist Veatch Program at Shelter Rock for
its generous support of the King Legacy series.

 In Association With

"The King Legacy" is a federally registered trademark of
the Unitarian Universalist Association Corporation.

Obvious typographical errors in transcriptions of spoken-word
materials were corrected to aid in ease of reading. All other errors or
stylistic inconsistencies have been retained in their original form.

Printed in the United States of America

15 14 13   8 7 6 5 4 3 2 1

Text design by Ralph L. Fowler

Library of Congress Cataloging-in-Publication data
can be found on page 248.

Contents

Reflection questions are included after each selection.

Young People Working for Justice

The Power of Freedom

Suffering, Hope, and the Future

Introduction
Martin Luther King, Jr.

I was seventeen in 1955 and a soldier in the United States Army. We had traveled from Massachusetts by train to Fort Polk, Louisiana. It was my first trip to the Deep South. I wasn't sure what to expect. I had heard about segregation, the forced separation of the races, but had only seen it in newspapers and on television. What was going on in Louisiana was a military exercise called Sage Brush. The Army was already involved in military operations in Vietnam, and the swampy terrain in southern Louisiana was considered to be the perfect training ground for continuing what was not yet being called a "war" overseas. Moreover, the Army wanted to test its new "Atomic Cannon," a weapon that would use nuclear ammunition for the first time. The theory was that the new artillery piece could fire nuclear shells that had little radioactive fallout, allowing foot soldiers to occupy the targeted areas and take the territory before an enemy could recover. I didn't know it at the time, but I was about to experience issues that would put our nation into turmoil for the next two decades—and would bring to prominence one of the most dynamic leaders of my lifetime, Dr. Martin Luther King, Jr.

When I arrived in Louisiana, when I saw what institutionalized racism was, I was shocked. Restaurant signs read "Whites Only" or "Colored Served in Rear." Some stores wouldn't serve black people, and there were movie houses in which they were made to sit in the balcony or, in some cases, not even permitted to enter.

Black children couldn't attend the same schools as their white friends and sometimes couldn't even play in the same parks. The signs did more than make me feel uncomfortable; they made me feel sick. I was being told that I wasn't as good as some people simply because of the color of my skin. And yet I was in the military, ready and willing to sacrifice my life for this country. When I boarded a bus I had to sit in the back, where people of my race were forced to sit. It made me feel ashamed to be black. I was told that these were the laws in this part of America, and I had to follow them.

Black people had protested segregation in the past. We had taken our cause to the courts and, for the most part, had been rejected. Most of the decisions had been based on an 1896 Supreme Court case (*Plessy v. Ferguson*), which stated that the equal protection clause of the Constitution was satisfied as long as the facilities for whites and blacks were "equal." But in May 1954, in a stunning decision, the Court declared that segregated schools were unconstitutional. The "separate but equal" ruling from the earlier decision had finally been reversed. For black people throughout the country, the ruling delivered in 1954 was an occasion for jubilation. We felt that segregation and the humiliation it brought would soon be over. We were wrong.

Although some white people spoke out against the segregated schools and facilities, most Southern leaders resisted the changes that they felt would lead to equality among the races. To many whites, there was definitely a "place" for blacks—who were also referred to at the time as Negroes or colored people—but that place was determined by tradition, and by the white race. Blacks understood that the struggle for our share in America's freedom had to be continued, but how? The Supreme Court had ruled that segregation was unconstitutional, but the resistance was so strong that no changes were being made—how could the Supreme Court's ruling be implemented and segregation actually dismantled? On Thursday, the first day of December 1955, a black woman boarded a bus in Montgomery, Alabama, and sat in the first available seat in the black section. As the bus filled, the white bus driver ordered her to relinquish the seat to a white passenger. Rosa Parks refused to move, and the driver called the police. Mrs. Parks was arrested and charged with breaking the law by refusing to be segregated, and she was ordered to pay a fine.

The issue for Rosa Parks was not simply that she was tired that day—she wasn't—or that segregation was embarrassing. A long-time activist, she understood what it meant to be a second-class citizen despite how hard she worked. She knew that black children were not getting the same kind of educational opportunities that white children were.

The National Association for the Advancement of Colored People (NAACP), an organization dedicated to the protection of human rights for black people, had been banned in Montgomery. In its place the Montgomery Improvement Association (MIA) had been formed. After Rosa Parks's arrest they met and decided to use her case to begin a protest against segregation in Montgomery.

Montgomery is a bustling, vital city and the capital of the state of Alabama. As a major Southern city, the rest of the country, it was thought, would certainly pay attention to what was going on there. Still, any protest had its risks. Although one-third of the Montgomery residents were black, they were among the poorest people in the city where the Confederate States of America had been formed in 1861. It was certain that a protest would result in a loss of precious jobs. The MIA wanted to press forward, but who would lead such a protest?

It couldn't be just the person who was angriest. Anger only produced a more violent reaction from authorities, and blacks had been beaten for protesting in the past. Many had even been killed. The leader had to be articulate, someone who could control his or her emotions and who could carry out a plan that would be effective. After considerable discussion, it was thought that a young minister, relatively new to the city, had all the qualifications needed. He was approached with the idea that he could lead a protest but warned that he might be physically injured or arrested, or that his home might be attacked and even his family would share the danger. After consulting with his wife, and asking God for guidance, the young minister accepted the challenge.

Martin Luther King, Jr., was born in Atlanta, Georgia, in 1929. The son of a Baptist minister, he finished high school at sixteen and completed his undergraduate work at Morehouse College in Atlanta before attending Crozer Theological Seminary in Pennsylvania. He then went to Boston University, where he received his doctorate degree, and in 1953, he married Coretta Scott, a student at the New England Conservatory of Music.

In 1955, the twenty-six-year-old minister was the pastor of the Drexel Avenue Baptist Church in Montgomery. When the MIA decided to protest segregation on the city's buses, it was this very young man they asked to be its spokesman.

The protest would have two main thrusts. The first was to explain and publicize the positions of black people in Montgomery. The MIA didn't think it was fair that a black person, once seated on a bus, would have to give up his or her seat solely because a city's law said that any white person was entitled to it. The second thrust was that, by refusing to ride the buses, protestors would exert economic pressure on the bus company to consider their black passengers with respect. Three-quarters of the people who rode the buses in Montgomery were black, and without them the bus company would have a difficult task maintaining its business.

The MIA quickly printed up circulars announcing the boycott. They organized car pools to bring people from their neighborhoods into the city to work. Some white employers also helped transport their employees into the city.

The reaction of some whites was equally quick—and very negative: Who were these people who wanted to change Montgomery's way of life? Why wouldn't they just continue as they had for years? The people who opposed the protest felt that they had more of a right to a good life than their black neighbors. Things had always been that way, they reasoned, so why change now? Montgomery mayor W. A. Gayle blamed the boycott on "Negro radicals."

Martin Luther King, Jr., was then only in his twenties, but when the newspapers and television cameras began interviewing him, they realized that he could state his position calmly, clearly, and eloquently. He said,

> The determination of the Negro himself to gain freedom and equality is the most powerful force that will ultimately defeat the barriers of integration.[1]

The city council believed that the boycott would not last. They thought that when it rained people would not want to walk to work. But it did rain, and still the boycott went on. The black people of Montgomery were determined to succeed. The protestors were called to a meeting by city officials and asked exactly what they wanted.

Dr. King said that they wanted three changes. The first was a first-come, first-served seating arrangement, with black people loading from the rear and whites loading from the front. Second, they wanted a guarantee of courtesy to all passengers, white and black, from the drivers. And third, since the bus company made so much money from the blacks of Birmingham, they wanted some black bus drivers to be hired, especially for routes through black neighborhoods.

Mayor Gayle said that Dr. King's requests were impossible to fulfill. They were against the laws of the state of Alabama, the mayor said, and he would be breaking the law if he granted Dr. King's wishes. When the boycott continued, Mayor Gayle went on local television and called for a "get tough" policy against the protestors. Many of the blacks who had been riding in private cars to their jobs in Montgomery were arrested. One of those arrested was Dr. King.

Dr. King was handled roughly during his arrest. When he was released he received threatening phone calls. But he realized that to give up the protest would be a great victory for those who worked against black rights. He insisted that everyone involved in the protest be polite to those who worked against them and not react to those who wanted to provoke them into some rash action.

But the sternest test of Dr. King's faith and personality was still to come. On a cold night in January, a bomb was thrown onto his front porch while he was attending a meeting. The bomb blew up as his wife, Coretta, their little child, and a neighbor were within.

Although relieved when he found out that his wife and child and the neighbor were unharmed, Dr. King was very upset. But he had the clarity of vision to understand that if he allowed violence to stop him, the aggressors would know that violence would work to stop black people from ending segregation, and more violence would be sure to follow. He said:

> Let us keep moving with the faith that what we are doing is
> right, and with the even greater faith that God is with us in
> the struggle.[2]

Rosa Parks was convicted, as expected, but a lawsuit challenging that conviction was started. The struggle was in the streets of Montgomery, but also in the courts.

The protest lasted a full year. In the meantime, another lawsuit brought by the MIA was making its way through the court system. This was a federal suit (*Browder v. Gayle*) claiming that some citizens of Montgomery had been denied the protection of the Constitution under the Fourteenth Amendment. One of the people involved in the case, fifteen-year-old Claudette Colvin, had refused to give up her seat and had been arrested, as Mrs. Parks had. "When it comes to justice, there is no easy way to get it. You can't sugarcoat it. You have to take a stand and say, 'This is not right,'" Ms. Colvin would say later when asked about her actions.[3]

The combination of Dr. King's tactics and the lawsuit brought by the MIA were extremely effective. Dr. King understood that the laws protecting segregation were often randomly applied and often misunderstood by people who lived outside of the states where segregation was a tradition. What he accomplished in the demonstrations he led was to show the world the brutality underlying the "'separate but equal'" doctrine. Southern newspapers often reported news about the protests in a way that was favorable to the local white community. But Dr. King saw that the then-new medium of television was showing segregation for what it really was. Day after day people across the United States were seeing peaceful, nonviolent people of color being harassed by young white toughs based purely on the color of their skin.

When reporters approached Dr. King, his responses to them were clear and straightforward. He said that people simply wanted the dignity and justice that all Americans deserved.

"What Dr. King has done," future Supreme Court justice Thurgood Marshall told me, as we sat in the offices of the NAACP Legal Defense Fund on a hot August day in 1959, "is to give a new direction and new energy to the civil rights movement. He's allowing people who were sitting on the sidelines to enter the movement with their support because he's taken the violence out of it."

The television coverage of the Montgomery boycott, along with the leadership of Dr. King, brought the issues before the American people as never before. Segregation was no longer something that happened to other people or behind closed doors in small Southern towns; it was being brought into living rooms across America. The image of fifteen-year-old Elizabeth Eckford walking alone through an angry, screaming crowd outside of Central High School in Little Rock, Arkansas, would bring a new vision of what segregation really meant and how much it could hurt, both emotionally and physically. Eckford was one of the black students called "the Little Rock Nine," who, lawfully, tried to integrate the previously all-white Arkansas high school. Not all of the abuse was restricted to name-calling. When it was discovered by the white protestors outside of the school that the nine black teenagers had actually entered the school building, the unruly mob began to break through the police protection to get to the frightened students.

"We were told to move very quickly, to go with dispatch to the basement where the [police] cars were waiting for us. They told us to put notebooks against the windows and keep down," said Terrence Roberts, one of the Little Rock Nine.[4]

Dr. King sent a telegram to President Eisenhower, asking him to "take a strong forthright stand in the Little Rock Situation."[5] In another telegram, to Little Rock minister Roland Smith and Daisy Bates, president of the Arkansas NAACP and advisor to the Little Rock Nine, Dr. King added:

> Urge the people of Little Rock to adhere rigorously to a way of non-violence at this time. I know this is difficult advice at a time when you are being terrorized, stoned, and threatened by ruthless mobs. But non-violence is the only way to a lasting solution of the problem.[6]

So, when *Browder v. Gayle* came before the Supreme Court, the issues were clear. The NAACP had grouped several cases together: those of Aurelia Browder, Susie McDonald, Mary Louise Smith, and Claudette Colvin, all women who had been arrested for not giving up their seats on public buses in Montgomery. In June 1956, the Supreme Court ruled in favor of the NAACP and said that Montgomery could not enforce segregation laws on public buses.

Understanding what had transpired in Montgomery, Dr. King widened his view of overcoming segregation. He, along with other civil rights leaders, formed the Southern Christian Leadership Conference. In doing so, Dr. King was greatly inspired by Mahatma Gandhi, the great Indian leader who had used nonviolent resistance and civil disobedience to overcome oppression in South Africa and India. Dr. King found that Gandhi's use of nonviolence resonated with his own religious beliefs in the power of love to unite all humankind.

Dr. King believed that the future of America was in the hearts and minds of its youth. He saw the fulfillment of his vision of our country in engaging young people in building and maintaining doctrines of fairness. And American youth of all races understood and responded to him.

The Freedom Riders were young men and women, black and white, who believed in universal justice and were willing to devote their time and put their lives on the line for their beliefs. Miriam Glickman was nineteen when she joined the Freedom Riders, taking a bus through the segregated South to test compliance with the new anti-segregation laws. A young white woman from a privileged background, she was beaten and jailed for maintaining her belief that all people are created equal.

Although the strategy of nonviolent protest was often personally risky and difficult for some, Dr. King was slowly convincing America that it would work. When the federal government stepped in and promised to protect peaceful demonstrations, activity both for and against the civil rights movement throughout the South increased. In the fall of 1960, two remarkable things happened. One was that a six-year-old girl, Ruby Bridges, became the first African American to attend a previously segregated school in New Orleans, Louisiana. The integration of the school was court ordered, and in response angry white parents kept their children out. Many gathered at the school and hooted and taunted the young girl. Ruby, nervous as she marched into the school and guarded each day by United States marshals, bravely attended the William Franz Elementary School nonetheless. Barbara Henry, a white teacher, not only taught Ruby but also became her best friend at the school. A short while later a white Methodist minister brought his little girl to school. Sometimes there were as many as twenty-eight white students attending school with Ruby, and at other times, as few as six. But eventually, the white boycott against the school ended, and the school was integrated. Again, the protest had been nonviolent, and it had been successful.

Dr. King's strategy was one of inclusion. He believed that most people had a sense of fairness and wanted justice. He felt that if he could reach these people, bring them out of their roles as spectators and enlist them in what he saw as the American dream, he would be more effective. He saw himself as leading a parade of Americans with good hearts and fair minds. His faith in the power of young people also continued to grow. It was still true that blacks had to fear the violence of people who hated them, as well as the loss of jobs and attacks on their families. As the numbers of people involved in the demonstrations began to increase, and as people around the nation and around the world saw how ordinary citizens were making a difference, Dr. King grew ever more hopeful. Soon there were nuns and teachers, folk singers and nurses, doctors and housewives joining the movement. Dr. King's stirring messages and his insistence on nonviolence were an inspiration to many across the nation.

In 1963 Dr. King moved his campaign to Birmingham, Alabama. In Birmingham, the head of public safety was a man by the name of T. Eugene "Bull" Connor. Mr. Connor, one of the most feared men in Birmingham, made it clear that he did not like blacks protesting and would do anything to stop it. He decided to answer the protests with violence. But Dr. King understood that Connor's open use of violence against peaceful, nonviolent demonstrators could help the cause of those fighting against segregation.

It was a brutal demonstration, but Dr. King understood what was going on much better than Bull Connor did. Connor thought that by using violence he could scare off supporters of the civil rights movement. Dr. King understood that few Americans of good conscience would look at armed policeman confronting young children in the streets of Birmingham or police dogs biting American citizens and fail to recognize that something was very wrong.

In May 1963, with the help of local Christian leaders, it was decided to bring a group of elementary, middle, and high school students into downtown Birmingham to speak with the mayor of that city. Over a thousand children and teenagers marched through the streets. They were followed by photographers and television cameras. When the Birmingham fire department turned their hoses on the youth, knocking some down in the streets, the scenes were played over and over on television sets around the world. The black people of Birmingham were suffering, but they were also winning the hearts and minds of the world.

Dr. King's enemies understood that, under this young minister's leadership, the country was beginning to change. Americans who had turned a blind eye to racial discrimination were now speaking up and, in some cases, were willing to march and protest along with the Southern Negroes.

As things changed, the opposition to civil rights became more pronounced. The Bull Connors of the Old South became more agitated and increased the violence. Many cities passed laws that required a permit to stage a demonstration. Dr. King had to worry about his own safety, the safety of the people he led, and that of his family. But there was an even greater threat to the movement. In July 1959, *News Beat*, a New York City television program, aired a documentary called *The Hate That Hate Produced*. The piece was about a black group based in Chicago that called itself the Nation of Islam and their leader, known as Malcolm X.

I had seen Malcolm X speaking on Harlem street corners. He was articulate and tall, and his words fired up crowds. To a large extent, what Malcolm X was saying made sense. He spoke of years of black enslavement and degradation. He pointed out the brutality of the reactions of the Ku Klux Klan and other white hate groups. But Malcolm X also ridiculed the efforts of Dr. King. "I've never heard of a non-violent revolution or a revolution that was brought about by turning the other cheek," he said.[7]

The Nation of Islam was a religious movement that had been founded in 1930 in Detroit, Michigan. Although it resembled the traditional Islam that was practiced in many other countries throughout the world, the Nation of Islam (or "black Muslims," as Dr. King and others sometimes referred to its adherents) was limited to black populations in the United States, largely in northern urban centers.

In their documentary, TV journalist Mike Wallace and African American journalist and author Louis Lomax showed thousands of followers of the Nation of Islam preaching the separation of the races. They also preached self-defense rather than passive resistance, as Dr. King did. The scenes of Birmingham firemen turning their hoses on protestors and allowing their dogs to bite people looking for equal rights should have been answered, Malcolm X said, with a show of determination. He argued that people had the right to defend themselves "by any means necessary."

Behind the arguments about whether to answer white oppression with violence or with Dr. King's nonviolence were two visions of what America would become. In Dr. King's vision, the country would become one great body in which all people would have the freedoms promised by the Founding Fathers. In the vision of the Nation of Islam and Malcolm X, black people needed to accept the idea of two Americas, one in which both whites and blacks had both powers and strengths, and in which they would interact only when it was mutually beneficial. The Nation of Islam was trying to help black people; Dr. King was trying to heal America.

In October 1964, Dr. King was awarded the Nobel Peace Prize, becoming the youngest person ever to receive that honor. The prize honors acts "for the furtherance of brotherhood among men and to the abolishment or reduction of standing armies and for the extension of these purposes."[8]

In 1967, the young minister—who had been chosen as a leader because he spoke well and because his vision of America encompassed the problems of the past but also the promise of the future—expanded that vision to include both the difficult war the United States was prosecuting in Vietnam and the issue of poverty in America. On April 30, 1967, Dr. King spoke at the Ebenezer Baptist Church in Atlanta about the war in Vietnam. He pointed out how much we were spending to support the war while Americans were suffering under conditions of poverty at home:

> We have been repeatedly faced with the cruel irony of watching Negro and white boys on TV screens as they kill and die together for a nation that has been unable to seat them together in the same schools.[9]

The early sixties saw the country in turmoil. The struggle to achieve civil rights was continuing, but the progress of the movement, under Dr. King, was steady. The country was changing its course, and the world saw it. Even after the assassination of President John Kennedy in November 1963, the movement continued forward. In 1964, President Lyndon Johnson signed the first civil rights legislation passed since 1868.

The debt we owe to Dr. Martin Luther King, Jr., is one that will live forever. He told a country that had tried to settle its racial problems with a devastating civil war, with bombings and lynching, with bloody riots in the cities that there was another way. Where those who argued for violence and retribution had specific methods in mind to overcome injustice, Dr. King had a vision for all of America that the entire nation could embrace. Today, his message resonates with as much clarity as it did more than fifty years ago as we continue to grapple with issues of racism and prejudice, poverty and war. What Dr. King preached, what he taught, was nonviolence to a nation seemingly intoxicated with violence. He taught inclusion to a nation that had incorporated separatism in its laws.

Dr. Martin Luther King, Jr., changed the world in which I lived. Today when I go to places like Little Rock, Montgomery, or New Orleans, I go without worrying about whether I will be accepted or where I can sit. I see children getting on buses and running for the first seat they see. I believe that if Dr. King were alive today, he would enlist an army of young people to help each other and America in the education process. He would trust them to bring their energy and sense of justice to end gang violence and to reverse the feeling of helplessness that hurts so many of our young people. He would keep marching against unjust laws, racism, war, and poverty. Dr. King made America a better place for all people to live during the turbulent years of the civil rights struggle. Using his insights, his courage in tackling difficult problems, and his loyalty to nonviolence both in action and in the language we use with each other, perhaps we can continue building the America he once thought possible. What do you think?

—Walter Dean Myers

Notes

1. From "A Look to the Future," address delivered at Highlander Folk School, Monteagle, Tennessee, in *The Papers of Martin Luther King, Jr.: Volume IV: Symbol of the Movement, January 1957-December 1958*, Clayborne Carson et al., eds. (Berkeley: University of California Press, 2000), 274.

2. *The Autobiography of Martin Luther King, Jr.*, Clayborne Carson, ed. (New York: Grand Central Publishing, reprint ed., 2001), 79.

3. Phillip Hoose, *Claudette Colvin: Twice Toward Justice* (New York: Farrar, Straus & Giroux, 2009), 104.

4. Terrence Roberts, *Lessons from Little Rock* (Little Rock: Butler Center for Arkansas Studies, 2009), 105.

5. September 9, 1957. In documents collection, Martin Luther King, Jr. Research and Education Institute, Stanford University.

6. September 26, 1957. In documents collection, Martin Luther King, Jr. Research and Education Institute, Stanford University.

7. A. B. Spellman, "Interview with Malcolm X," from March 19, 1964, in *Monthly Review* 56, no. 9 (February 2005), http://monthlyreview.org/2005/02/01/interview-with-malcolm-x.

8. "Martin Luther King Wins The Nobel Prize for Peace," *New York Times*, October 14, 1964.

9. From "Conscience and the Vietnam War," 1967, delivered as part of the Massey Lecture Series, Canadian Broadcasting Company. In Martin Luther King, Jr., *The Trumpet of Conscience* (Boston: Beacon Press, 2010), 23.

A Time
to Break
Silence

Love and Faith

A Gift of Love

In this 1966 sermon, part of a Christmas series, Dr. King calls non-violence one of the most important gifts of love. He also uses the term "Freedom Movement" to broaden listeners' understanding of the multiple goals and varying strategies of black activists beyond the effort to achieve national civil rights legislation. By the time Dr. King delivered this sermon, he and his supporters had expanded their activities from the South to Northern cities, where racial oppression resulted more from institutional practices than from overt racism and discriminatory laws.

This Christmas I remember the little black children of Grenada, Mississippi, beaten by grown men as they walked to school. I remember a baby, attacked by rats in a Chicago slum. I remember a young Negro, murdered by a gang in Cicero, Illinois, where he was looking for a job; and a white minister in Georgia, forced out of his sacred office because he spoke for human dignity. I remember, too, farm workers in Mississippi, risking their lives and their livelihood to march out of the cotton fields and vote for freedom and democracy.

This I remember, especially in this season of giving, for these people have followed the example and spirit of Christ Himself. They have given mankind a priceless "Gift of Love."

Originally published in McCall's *(December 1966).*

I am thinking now of some teenage boys in Chicago. They have nicknames like "Tex," and "Pueblo," and "Goat," and "Teddy." They hail from the Negro slums. Forsaken by society, they once proudly fought and lived for street gangs like the Vice Lords, the Roman Saints, the Rangers.

But this year, they gave us all the gift of nonviolence, which is indeed a gift of love.

I met these boys and heard their stories in discussions we had on some long, cold nights last winter at the slum apartment I rent in the West Side ghetto of Chicago. I was shocked at the venom they poured out against the world. At times I shared their despair and felt a hopelessness that these young Americans could ever embrace the concept of nonviolence as the effective and powerful instrument of social reform.

All their lives, boys like this have known life as a madhouse of violence and degradation. Some have never experienced a meaningful family life. Some have police records. Some dropped out of the incredibly bad slum schools, then were deprived of honorable work, then took to the streets.

To the young victim of the slums, this society has so limited the alternatives of his life that the expression of his manhood is reduced to the ability to defend himself physically. No wonder it appears logical to him to strike out, resorting to violence against oppression. That is the only way he thinks he can get recognition.

And so, we have seen occasional rioting—and, much more frequently and consistently, brutal acts and crimes by Negroes against Negroes. In many a week in Chicago, as many or more Negro youngsters have been killed in gang fights as were killed in the riots there last summer.

The Freedom Movement has tried to bring a message to boys like Tex. First, we explained that violence can be put down by armed might and police work, that physical force can never solve the underlying social problems. Second, we promised them we could prove, by example, that nonviolence works.

The young slum dweller has good reason to be suspicious of promises. But these young people in Chicago agreed last winter to give nonviolence a test. Then came the very long, very tense, hot summer of 1966, and the first test for many Chicago youngsters: the Freedom March through Mississippi. Gang members went there in carloads.

Those of us who had been in the movement for years were apprehensive about the behavior of the boys. Before the march ended, they were to be attacked by tear gas. They were to be called upon to protect women and children on the march, with no other weapon than their own bodies. To them, it would be a strange and possibly nonsensical way to respond to violence.

But they reacted splendidly! They learned in Mississippi, and returned to teach in Chicago, the beautiful lesson of acting against evil by renouncing force.

And in Chicago, the test was sterner. These marchers endured not only the filthiest kind of verbal abuse, but also barrages of rocks and sticks and eggs and cherry bombs. They did not reply in words or violent deeds. Once again, their only weapon was their own bodies. I saw boys like Goat leap into the air to catch with their bare hands the bricks and bottles that were sailed toward us.

It was through the Chicago marches that our promise to them— that nonviolence achieves results—was redeemed, and their hopes for a better life were rekindled. For they saw, in Chicago, that a humane police force—in contrast to police in Mississippi—could defend the exercise of constitutional rights as well as enforce the law in the ghetto.

They saw, in prosperous white American communities, that hatred and bigotry could and should be confronted, exposed, and dealt with. They saw, in the very heart of a great city, that men of power could be made to listen to the tramp of marching feet and the call for freedom and justice, and use their power to work for a truly Open City for all.

Boys like Teddy, a child of the slums, saw all this because they decided to rise above the cruelties of those slums and to work and march, peacefully, for human dignity. They revitalized my own faith in nonviolence. And these poverty-stricken boys enriched us all with a gift of love.

Reflection Questions

1. Dr. King calls nonviolence a gift of love. What does this determination suggest about the relationship between the two?

2. How does Dr. King convince the reader to think differently about young men in urban areas? What does he find them capable of achieving?

3. What parallels do you notice between the places Dr. King describes in his essay and the present day? What lessons can we apply from this essay to modern-day challenges?

4. Dr. King invests much hope in young people in this essay. Why do you think this is the case?

An Experiment in Love

The concept of *agape*—which Dr. King defined as "the love of God operating in the human heart"—was central to his understanding of nonviolent resistance and creating a global "beloved community." In the following essay, Dr. King explains how *agape* undergirds nonviolent resistance to injustice.

From the beginning a basic philosophy guided the movement. This guiding principle has since been referred to variously as nonviolent resistance, noncooperation, and passive resistance. But in the first days of the protest none of these expressions was mentioned: the phrase most often heard was "Christian love." It was the Sermon on the Mount, rather than a doctrine of passive resistance, that initially inspired the Negroes of Montgomery to dignified social action. It was Jesus of Nazareth that stirred the Negroes to protest with the creative weapon of love.

As the days unfolded, however, the inspiration of Mahatma Gandhi began to exert its influence. I had come to see early that the Christian doctrine of love operating through the Gandhian method of nonviolence was one of the most potent weapons available to the Negro in his struggle for freedom. About a week after the protest started, a white woman

Originally published in Jubilee *(September 1958) as an excerpt from* Stride Toward Freedom: The Montgomery Story *(New York: Harper & Brothers, 1958, reprinted by Beacon Press).*

who understood and sympathized with the Negroes' efforts wrote a letter to the editor of the *Montgomery Advertiser* comparing the bus protest with the Gandhian movement in India. Miss Juliette Morgan, sensitive and frail, did not long survive the rejection and condemnation of the white community, but long after she died in the summer of 1957 the name of Mahatma Gandhi was well known in Montgomery. People who had never heard of the little brown saint of India were now saying his name with an air of familiarity. Nonviolent resistance had emerged as the technique of the movement, while love stood as the regulating ideal. In other words, Christ furnished the spirit and motivation, while Gandhi furnished the method.

One of the glories of the Montgomery movement was that Baptists, Methodists, Lutherans, Presbyterians, Episcopalians, and others all came together with a willingness to transcend denominational lines. Although no Catholic priests were actively involved in the protest, many of their parishioners took part. All joined hands in the bond of Christian love. Thus the mass meetings accomplished on Monday and Thursday nights what the Christian Church had failed to accomplish on Sunday mornings.

In my weekly remarks as president of the resistance committee, I stressed that the use of violence in our struggle would be both impractical and immoral. To meet hate with retaliatory hate would do nothing but intensify the existence of evil in the universe. Hate begets hate; violence begets violence; toughness begets a greater toughness. We must meet the forces of hate with the power of love; we must meet physical force with soul force. Our aim must never be to defeat or humiliate the white man, but to win his friendship and understanding.

In a real sense, Montgomery's Negroes showed themselves willing to grapple with a new approach to the crisis in race relations. It is probably true that most of them did not believe in nonviolence as a philosophy of life, but because of their confidence in their leaders and because nonviolence was presented to them as a simple expression of Christianity in action, they were willing to use it as a technique. Admittedly, nonviolence in the truest sense is not a strategy that one uses simply because it is expedient at the moment; nonviolence is ultimately a way of life that men live by because of the sheer morality of its claim. But even granting this, the willingness to use nonviolence as a technique is a step forward. For he who goes this far is more likely to adopt nonviolence later as a way of life.

It must be emphasized that nonviolent resistance is not a method for cowards; it does resist. If one uses this method because he is afraid or merely because he lacks the instruments of violence, he is not truly nonviolent. This is why Gandhi often said that if cowardice is the only alternative to violence, it is better to fight. He made this statement conscious of the fact that there is always another alternative: no individual or group need submit to any wrong, nor need they use violence to right that wrong; there is the way of nonviolent resistance. This is ultimately the way of the strong man. It is not a method of stagnant passivity. The phrase "passive resistance" often gives the false impression that this is a sort of "do-nothing method" in which the resister quietly and passively accepts evil. But nothing is further from the truth. For while the nonviolent resister is passive in the sense that he is not physically aggressive toward his opponent, his mind and emotions are always active, constantly seeking to persuade his opponent that he is wrong. The method is passive physically but strongly active spiritually. It is not passive nonresistance to evil, it is active nonviolent resistance to evil.

A second basic fact that characterizes nonviolence is that it does not seek to defeat or humiliate the opponent, but to win his friendship and understanding. The nonviolent resister must often express his protest through noncooperation or boycotts, but he realizes that these are not ends themselves; they are merely means to awaken a sense of moral shame in the opponent. The end is redemption and reconciliation. The aftermath of nonviolence is the creation of the beloved community, while the aftermath of violence is tragic bitterness.

A third characteristic of this method is that the attack is directed against forces of evil rather than against persons who happen to be doing the evil. It is evil that the nonviolent resister seeks to defeat, not the persons victimized by evil. If he is opposing racial injustice, the nonviolent resister has the vision to see that the basic tension is not between races. As I like to say to the people in Montgomery: "The tension in this city is not between white people and Negro people. The tension is, at bottom, between justice and injustice, between the forces of light and the forces of darkness. And if there is a victory, it will be a victory not merely for fifty thousand Negroes, but a victory for justice and the forces of light. We are out to defeat injustice and not white persons who may be unjust."

A fourth point that characterizes nonviolent resistance is a willingness to accept suffering without retaliation, to accept blows from the opponent without striking back. "Rivers of blood may have to flow before we gain our freedom, but it must be our blood," Gandhi said to his countrymen. The nonviolent resister is willing to accept violence if necessary, but never to inflict it. He does not seek to dodge jail. If going to jail is necessary, he enters it "as a bridegroom enters the bride's chamber."

One may well ask: "What is the nonviolent resister's justification for this ordeal to which he invites men, for this mass political application of the ancient doctrine of turning the other cheek?" The answer is found in the realization that unearned suffering is redemptive. Suffering, the nonviolent resister realizes, has tremendous educational and transforming possibilities. "Things of fundamental importance to people are not secured by reason alone, but have to be purchased with their suffering," said Gandhi. He continues: "Suffering is infinitely more powerful than the law of the jungle for converting the opponent and opening his ears which are otherwise shut to the voice of reason."

A fifth point concerning nonviolent resistance is that it avoids not only external physical violence but also internal violence of spirit. The nonviolent resister not only refuses to shoot his opponent but he also refuses to hate him. At the center of nonviolence stands the principle of love. The nonviolent resister would contend that in the struggle for human dignity, the oppressed people of the world must not succumb to the temptation of becoming bitter or indulging in hate campaigns. To retaliate in kind would do nothing but intensify the existence of hate in the universe. Along the way of life, someone must have sense enough and morality enough to cut off the chain of hate. This can only be done by projecting the ethic of love to the center of our lives.

In speaking of love at this point, we are not referring to some sentimental or affectionate emotion. It would be nonsense to urge men to love their oppressors in an affectionate sense. Love in this connection means understanding, redemptive good will. When we speak of loving those who oppose us, we refer to neither *eros* nor *philia*; we speak of a love which is expressed in the Greek word *agape*. *Agape* means understanding, redeeming good will for all men. It is an overflowing love which is purely spontaneous, unmotivated, groundless, and creative. It is not set in motion by any quality or function of its object. It is the love of God operating in the human heart.

Agape is disinterested love. It is a love in which the individual seeks not his own good, but the good of his neighbor (1 Corinthians 10:24). *Agape* does not begin by discriminating between worthy and unworthy people, or any qualities people possess. It begins by loving others *for their sakes*. It is an entirely "neighbor-regarding concern for others," which discovers the neighbor in every man it meets. Therefore, *agape* makes no distinction between friend and enemy; it is directed toward both. If one loves an individual merely on account of his friendliness, he loves him for the sake of the benefits to be gained from the friendship, rather than for the friend's own sake. Consequently, the best way to assure oneself that love is disinterested is to have love for the enemy-neighbor from whom you can expect no good in return, only hostility and persecution.

Another basic point about *agape* is that it springs from the *need* of the other person—his need for belonging to the best in the human family. The Samaritan who helped the Jew on the Jericho Road was "good" because he responded to the human need that he was presented with. God's love is eternal and fails not because man needs his love. Saint Paul assures us that the loving act of redemption was done "while we were yet sinners"—that is, at the point of our greatest need for love. Since the white man's personality is greatly distorted by segregation, and his soul is greatly scarred, he needs the love of the Negro. The Negro must love the white man, because the white man needs his love to remove his tensions, insecurities, and fears.

Agape is not a weak, passive love. It is love in action. *Agape* is love seeking to preserve and create community. It is insistence on community even when one seeks to break it. *Agape* is a willingness to go to any length to restore community. It doesn't stop at the first mile, but it goes the second mile to restore community. It is a willingness to forgive, not seven times, but seventy times seven to restore community. The cross is the eternal expression of the length to which God will go in order to restore broken community. The resurrection is a symbol of God's triumph over all the forces that seek to block community. The Holy Spirit is the continuing community creating reality that moves through history. He who works against community is working against the whole of creation. Therefore, if I respond to hate with a reciprocal hate I do nothing but intensify the cleavage in broken community. I can only close the gap in broken community by meeting hate with love. If I meet hate with hate, I become depersonalized, because creation is so designed that my personality can only be fulfilled in the context of community. Booker T. Washington was right: "Let no man pull you so low as to make you hate him." When he pulls you that low he brings you to the point of working against community; he drags you to the point of defying creation, and thereby becoming depersonalized.

In the final analysis, *agape* means a recognition of the fact that all life is interrelated. All humanity is involved in a single process, and all men are brothers. To the degree that I harm my brother, no matter what he is doing to me, to that extent I am harming myself. For example, white men often refuse federal aid to education in order to avoid giving the Negro his rights; but because all men are brothers they cannot deny Negro children without harming their own. They end, all efforts to the contrary, by hurting themselves. Why is this? Because men are brothers. If you harm me, you harm yourself.

A sixth basic fact about nonviolent resistance is that it is based on the conviction that the universe is on the side of justice. Consequently, the believer in nonviolence has deep faith in the future. This faith is another reason why the nonviolent resister can accept suffering without retaliation. For he knows that in his struggle for justice he has cosmic companionship. It is true that there are devout believers in nonviolence who find it difficult to believe in a personal God. But even these persons believe in the existence of some creative force that works for universal wholeness. Whether we call it an unconscious process, an impersonal Brahman, or a Personal Being of matchless power and infinite love, there is a creative force in this universe that works to bring the disconnected aspects of reality into a harmonious whole.

Reflection Questions

1. What are the six characteristics of nonviolent resistance that Dr. King outlines? What are the key elements of each and what are the reasons Dr. King gives for each one? Which aspect do you think would be easiest to practice? Which would be hardest? Explain why.

2. Distinguish between what Dr. King calls "nonviolence as a strategy" versus "nonviolence as a way of life." How is one more powerful than the other?

3. How is nonviolent resistance active and not passive? Why might it be difficult to think of nonviolent resistance as active?

4. What is *agape*? How is *agape* different from the way we tend to use the word *love* in the English language? What is the significance of Dr. King's argument for *agape*?

5. Dr. King says that nonviolent resistance is not for cowards. Why is it courageous to practice nonviolence?

Loving Your Enemies

Convicted in July 1962 for participating in Albany Movement demonstrations the previous December, Dr. King and his close friend and movement colleague Ralph Abernathy refused to pay their fines and announced instead that they would serve forty-five-day jail terms. After spending two nights in a jail that Dr. King described as "dirty, filthy and ill-equipped ... [the] worst I have ever seen," the two men were unexpectedly bailed out by an unidentified black man. "This was one time that I was out of jail and I was not happy to be out," Dr. King commented.* When he was again jailed later in July, Dr. King used his two weeks of imprisonment to revise one of his favorite sermons, "Loving Your Enemies," for inclusion in the sermon book *Strength to Love*, which was published in 1963. Dr. King insisted that loving one's enemies could bring about conversion and dialogue.

So I want to turn your attention to this subject: "Loving Your Enemies." It's so basic to me because it is a part of my basic philosophical and theological orientation—the whole idea of love, the whole philosophy of love. In the fifth chapter of the gospel as recorded

Autobiography of Martin Luther King, Jr., Clayborne Carson, ed. (New York: Grand Central Publishing, reprint ed., 2001), 159.

Delivered at Dexter Avenue Baptist Church, Montgomery, Alabama, November 17, 1957. This version published in A Knock at Midnight: Inspiration from the Great Sermons of Martin Luther King, Jr., *eds. Clayborne Carson and Peter Holloran (New York: Warner Books, 2000).*

by Saint Matthew, we read these very arresting words flowing from the lips of our Lord and Master: "Ye have heard that it has been said, 'Thou shall love thy neighbor, and hate thine enemy.' But I say unto you, 'Love your enemies, bless them that curse you, do good to them that hate you, and pray for them that despitefully use you, that ye may be the children of your Father which is in heaven.'"

Certainly these are great words, words lifted to cosmic proportions. And over the centuries, many persons have argued that this is an extremely difficult command. Many would go so far as to say that it just isn't possible to move out into the actual practice of this glorious command. They would go on to say that this is just additional proof that Jesus was an impractical idealist who never quite came down to earth. So the arguments abound. But far from being an impractical idealist, Jesus has become the practical realist. The words of this text glitter in our eyes with a new urgency. Far from being the pious injunction of a utopian dreamer, this command is an absolute necessity for the survival of our civilization. Yes, it is love that will save our world and our civilization, love even for enemies.

Now let me hasten to say that Jesus was very serious when he gave this command; he wasn't playing. He realized that it's hard to love your enemies. He realized that it's difficult to love those persons who seek to defeat you, those persons who say evil things about you. He realized that it was painfully hard, pressingly hard. But he wasn't playing. And we cannot dismiss this passage as just another example of Oriental hyperbole, just a sort of exaggeration to get over the point. This is a basic philosophy of all that we hear coming from the lips of our Master. Because Jesus wasn't playing; because he was serious. We have the Christian and moral responsibility to seek to discover the meaning of these words, and to discover how we can live out this command, and why we should live by this command.

Now, first let us deal with this question, which is the practical question: How do you go about loving your enemies? I think the first thing is this: In order to love your enemies, you must begin by analyzing [your] self. And I'm sure that seems strange to you, that I start out telling you this morning that you love your enemies by beginning with a look at [your]self. It seems to me that that is the first and foremost way to come to an adequate discovery to the how of this situation.

Now, I'm aware of the fact that some people will not like you, not because of something you have done to them, but they just won't like you. I'm quite aware of that. Some people aren't going to like the way you walk; some people aren't going to like the way you talk. Some people aren't going to like you because you can do your job better than they can do theirs. Some people aren't going to like you because other people like you, and because you're popular, and because you're well-liked, they aren't going to like you. Some people aren't going to like you because your hair is a little shorter than theirs or your hair is a little longer than theirs. Some people aren't going to like you because your skin is a little brighter than theirs, and others aren't going to like you because your skin is a little darker than theirs. So that some people aren't going to like you. They're going to dislike you, not because of something that you've done to them, but because of various jealous reactions and other reactions that are so prevalent in human nature.

But after looking at these things and admitting these things, we must face the fact that an individual might dislike us because of something that we've done deep down in the past, some personality attribute that we possess, something that we've done deep down in the past and we've forgotten about it; but it was that something that aroused the hate response within the individual. That is why I say, begin with yourself. There might be something within you that arouses the tragic hate response in the other individual.

This is true in our international struggle. We look at the struggle, the ideological struggle between communism on the one hand and democracy on the other, and we see the struggle between America and Russia. Now certainly, we can never give our allegiance to the Russian way of life, to the communistic way of life, because communism is based on an ethical relativism and a metaphysical materialism that no Christian can accept. When we look at the methods of communism, a philosophy where somehow the end justifies the means, we cannot accept that because we believe as Christians that the end is pre-existent in the means. But in spite of all of the weaknesses and evils inherent in communism, we must at the same time see the weaknesses and evils within democracy.

Democracy is the greatest form of government to my mind that man has ever conceived, but the weakness is that we have never touched it. Isn't it true that we have often taken necessities from the masses to give luxuries to the classes? Isn't it true that we have often in our democracy trampled over individuals and races with the iron feet of oppression? Isn't it true that through our Western powers we have perpetuated colonialism and imperialism? And all of these things must be taken under consideration as we look at Russia. We must face the fact that the rhythmic beat of the deep rumblings of discontent from Asia and Africa is at bottom a revolt against the imperialism and colonialism perpetuated by Western civilization all these many years. The success of communism in the world today is due to the failure of democracy to live up to the noble ideals and principles inherent in its system.

And this is what Jesus means when he said: "How is it that you can see the mote in your brother's eye and not see the beam in your own eye?" Or to put it in [James] Moffatt's translation: "How is it that you see the splinter in your brother's eye and fail to see the plank in your own eye?" And this is one of the tragedies of human nature. So we begin to love our enemies and love those persons that hate us whether in collective life or individual life by looking at ourselves.

A second thing that an individual must do in seeking to love his enemy is to discover the element of good in his enemy, and every time you begin to hate that person and think of hating that person, realize that there is some good there and look at those good points which will over-balance the bad points.

I've said to you on many occasions that each of us is something of a schizophrenic personality. We're split up and divided against ourselves.

And there is something of a civil war going on within all of our lives. There is a recalcitrant South of our soul revolting against the North of our soul. And there is this continual struggle within the very structure of every individual life. There is something within all of us that causes us to cry out with Ovid, the Latin poet, "I see and approve the better things of life, but the evil things I do." There is something within all of us that causes us to cry out with Plato that the human personality is like a charioteer with two headstrong horses, each wanting to go in different directions. There is something within each of us that causes us to cry out with Goethe, "There is enough stuff in me to make both a gentleman and a rogue." There is something within each of us that causes us to cry out with Apostle Paul, "I see and approve the better things of life, but the evil things I do."

So somehow the "isness" of our present nature is out of harmony with the eternal "oughtness" that forever confronts us. And this simply means this: That within the best of us, there is some evil, and within the worst of us, there is some good. When we come to see this, we take a different attitude toward individuals. The person who hates you most has some good in him; even the nation that hates you most has some good in it; even the race that hates you most has some good in it. And when you come to the point that you look in the face of every man and see deep down within him what religion calls "the image of God," you begin to love him in spite of . . . no matter what he does, you see God's image there. There is an element of goodness that he can never slough off. Discover the element of good in your enemy. And as you seek to hate him, find the center of goodness and place your attention there and you will take a new attitude.

Another way that you love your enemy is this: When the opportunity presents itself for you to defeat your enemy, that is the time which you must not do it. There will come a time, in many instances, when the person who hates you most, the person who has misused you most, the person who has gossiped about you most, the person who has spread false rumors about you most, there will come a time when you will have an opportunity to defeat that person. It might be in terms of a recommendation for a job; it might be in terms of helping that person to make some move in life. That's the time you must do it. That is the meaning of love. In the final analysis, love is not this sentimental something that we talk about. It's not merely an emotional something. Love is creative, understanding goodwill for all men. It is the refusal to defeat any individual. When you rise to the level of love, of its great beauty and power, you seek only to defeat evil systems. Individuals who happen to be caught up in that system, you love, but you seek to defeat the system.

The Greek language, as I've said so often before, is very powerful at this point. It comes to our aid beautifully in giving us the real meaning and depth of the whole philosophy of love. And I think it is quite apropos at this point, for you see the Greek language has three words for love, interestingly enough. It talks about love as *eros*. That's one word for love. *Eros* is a sort of aesthetic love. Plato talks about it a great deal in his dialogues, a sort of yearning of the soul for the realm of the gods. And it's come to us to be a sort of romantic love, though it's a beautiful love. Everybody has experienced *eros* in all of its beauty when you find some individual that is attractive to you and that you pour out all of your like and your love on that individual. That is *eros*, you see, and it's a powerful, beautiful love that is given to us through all of the beauty of literature; we read about it.

Then the Greek language talks about *philia*, and that's another type of love that's also beautiful. It is a sort of intimate affection between personal friends. And this is the type of love that you have for those persons that you're friendly with—your intimate friends, or people that you call on the telephone and you go by to have dinner with, and your roommate in college and that type of thing. It's a sort of reciprocal love. On this level, you like a person because that person likes you. You love on this level, because you are loved. You love on this level, because there's something about the person you love that is likeable to you. This too is a beautiful love. You can communicate with a person; you have certain things in common; you like to do things together. This is *philia*.

The Greek language comes out with another word for love. It is the word *agape*. And *agape* is more than *eros*; *agape* is more than *philia*; *agape* is something of the understanding, creative, redemptive goodwill for all men. It is a love that seeks nothing in return. It is an overflowing love; it's what theologians would call the love of God working in the lives of men. And when you rise to love on this level, you begin to love men, not because they are likeable, but because God loves them. You look at every man, and you love him because you know God loves him. And he might be the worst person you've ever seen.

And this is what Jesus means, I think, in this very passage when he says, "Love your enemy." And it's significant that he does not say, "*Like* your enemy." *Like* is a sentimental something, an affectionate something. There are a lot of people that I find it difficult to like. I don't like what they do to me. I don't like what they say about me and other people. I don't like their attitudes. I don't like some of the things they're doing. I don't like them. But Jesus says love them. And *love* is greater than *like*. *Love* is understanding, redemptive goodwill for all men, so that you love everybody, because God loves them. You refuse to do anything that will defeat an individual, because you have *agape* in your soul. And here you come to the point that you love the individual who does the evil deed while hating the deed that the person does. This is what Jesus means when he says, "Love your enemy." This is the way to do it. When the opportunity presents itself when you can defeat your enemy, you must not do it.

Now for the few moments left, let us move from the practical how to the theoretical why. It's not only necessary to know how to go about loving your enemies, but also to go down into the question of why we should love our enemies. I think the first reason that we should love our enemies, and I think this was at the very center of Jesus' thinking, is this: that hate for hate only intensifies the existence of hate and evil in the universe. If I hit you and you hit me and I hit you back and you hit me back and go on, you see, that goes on ad infinitum. It just never ends. Somewhere somebody must have a little sense, and that's the strong person. The strong person is the person who can cut off the chain of hate, the chain of evil. And that is the tragedy of hate, that it doesn't cut it off. It only intensifies the existence of hate and evil in the universe. Somebody must have religion enough and morality enough to cut it off and inject within the very structure of the universe that strong and powerful element of love.

I think I mentioned before that sometime ago my brother and I were driving one evening to Chattanooga, Tennessee, from Atlanta. He was driving the car. And for some reason the drivers were very discourteous that night. They didn't dim their lights; hardly any driver that passed by dimmed his lights. And I remember very vividly, my brother A. D. looked over and in a tone of anger said: "I know what I'm going to do. The next car that comes along here and refuses to dim the lights, I'm going to fail to dim mine and pour them on in all of their power." And I looked at him right quick and said: "Oh no, don't do that. There'd be too much light on this highway, and it will end up in mutual destruction for all. Somebody got to have some sense on this highway."

Somebody must have sense enough to dim the lights, and that is the trouble, isn't it? That as all of the civilizations of the world move up the highway of history, so many civilizations, having looked at other civilizations that refused to dim the lights, and they decided to refuse to dim theirs. And Toynbee tells that out of the twenty-two civilizations that have risen up, all but about seven have found themselves in the junkheap of destruction. It is because civilizations fail to have sense enough to dim the lights. And if somebody doesn't have sense enough to turn on the dim and beautiful and powerful lights of love in this world, the whole of our civilization will be plunged into the abyss of destruction. And we will all end up destroyed because nobody had any sense on the highway of history. Somewhere somebody must have some sense. Men must see that force begets force, hate begets hate, toughness begets toughness. And it is all a descending spiral, ultimately ending in destruction for all and everybody. Somebody must have sense enough and morality enough to cut off the chain of hate and the chain of evil in the universe. And you do that by love.

There's another reason why you should love your enemies, and that is because hate distorts the personality of the hater. We usually think of what hate does for the individual hated or the individuals hated or the groups hated. But it is even more tragic, it is even more ruinous and injurious to the individual who hates. You just begin hating somebody, and you will begin to do irrational things. You can't see straight when you hate. You can't walk straight when you hate. You can't stand upright. Your vision is distorted. There is nothing more tragic than to see an individual whose heart is filled with hate. He comes to the point that he becomes a pathological case. For the person who hates, you can stand up and see a person and that person can be beautiful, and you will call them ugly. For the person who hates, the beautiful becomes ugly and the ugly becomes beautiful. For the person who hates, the good becomes bad and the bad becomes good. For the person who hates, the true becomes false and the false becomes true. That's what hate does. You can't see right. The symbol of objectivity is lost. Hate destroys the very structure of the personality of the hater. And this is why Jesus says hate [does damage to the self] *[Recording interrupted]* ...

... The way to be integrated with yourself is be sure that you meet every situation of life with an abounding love. Never hate, because it ends up in tragic, neurotic responses. Psychologists and psychiatrists are telling us today that the more we hate, the more we develop guilt feelings and we begin to subconsciously repress or consciously suppress certain emotions, and they all stack up in our subconscious selves and make for tragic, neurotic responses. And may this not be the neuroses of many individuals as they confront life that that is an element of hate there. And modern psychology is calling on us now to love. But long before modern psychology came into being, the world's greatest psychologist who walked around the hills of Galilee told us to love. He looked at men and said: "Love your enemies; don't hate anybody." It's not enough for us to hate your friends because—to love your friends—because when you start hating anybody, it destroys the very center of your creative response to life and the universe; so love everybody. Hate at any point is a cancer that gnaws away at the very vital center of your life and your existence. It is like eroding acid that eats away the best and the objective center of your life. So Jesus says love, because hate destroys the hater as well as the hated.

Now there is a final reason I think that Jesus says, "Love your enemies." It is this: that love has within it a redemptive power. And there is a power there that eventually transforms individuals. That's why Jesus says, "Love your enemies." Because if you hate your enemies, you have no way to redeem and to transform your enemies. But if you love your enemies, you will discover that at the very root of love is the power of redemption. You just keep loving people and keep loving them, even though they're mistreating you. Here's the person who is a neighbor, and this person is doing something wrong to you and all of that. Just keep being friendly to that person. Keep loving them. Don't do anything to embarrass them. Just keep loving them, and they can't stand it too long. Oh, they react in many ways in the beginning. They react with bitterness because they're mad because you love them like that. They react with guilt feelings, and sometimes they'll hate you a little more at that transition period, but just keep loving them. And by the power of your love they will break down under the load. That's love, you see. It is redemptive, and this is why Jesus says love. There's something about love that builds up and is creative. There is something about hate that tears down and is destructive. So love your enemies.

I think of one of the best examples of this. We all remember the great president of this United States, Abraham Lincoln—these United States rather. You remember when Abraham Lincoln was running for president of the United States, there was a man who ran all around the country talking about Lincoln. He said a lot of bad things about Lincoln, a lot of unkind things. And sometimes he would get to the point that he would even talk about his looks, saying, "You don't want a tall, lanky, ignorant man like this as the president of the United States." He went on and on and went around with that type of attitude and wrote about it. Finally, one day Abraham Lincoln was elected president of the United States. And if you read the great biography of Lincoln, if you read the great works about him, you will discover that as every president comes to the point, he came to the point of having to choose a Cabinet. And then came the time for him to choose a secretary of war. He looked across the nation, and decided to choose a man by the name of Mr. Stanton. And when Abraham Lincoln stood around his advisors and mentioned this fact, they said to him: "Mr. Lincoln, are you a fool? Do you know what Mr. Stanton has been saying about you? Do you know what he has done, tried to do to you? Do you know that he has tried to defeat you on every hand? Do you know that, Mr. Lincoln? Did you read all of those derogatory statements that he made about you?" Abraham Lincoln stood before the advisors around him and said: "Oh yes, I know about it; I read about it; I've heard him myself. But after looking over the country, I find that he is the best man for the job."

Mr. Stanton did become secretary of war, and ... later, Abraham Lincoln was assassinated. And if you go to Washington, you will discover that one of the greatest words or statements ever made about Abraham Lincoln was made [by] this man Stanton. And as Abraham Lincoln came to the end of his life, Stanton stood up and said: "Now he belongs to the ages." And he made a beautiful statement concerning the character and the stature of this man. If Abraham Lincoln had hated Stanton, if Abraham Lincoln had answered everything Stanton said, Abraham Lincoln would have not transformed and redeemed Stanton. Stanton would have gone to his grave hating Lincoln, and Lincoln would have gone to his grave hating Stanton. But through the power of love Abraham Lincoln was able to redeem Stanton.

That's it. There is a power in love that our world has not discovered yet. Jesus discovered it centuries ago. Mahatma Gandhi of India discovered it a few years ago, but most men and most women never discover it. For they believe in hitting for hitting; they believe in an eye for an eye and a tooth for a tooth; they believe in hating for hating; but Jesus comes to us and says, "This isn't the way."

And oh this morning, as I think of the fact that our world is in transition now, our whole world is facing a revolution. Our nation is facing a revolution, our nation. One of the things that concerns me most is that in the midst of the revolution of the world and the midst of the revolution of this nation, that we will discover the meaning of Jesus' words.

History unfortunately leaves some people oppressed and some people oppressors. And there are three ways that individuals who are oppressed can deal with their oppression. One of them is to rise up against their oppressors with physical violence and corroding hatred. But oh, this isn't the way. For the danger and the weakness of this method is its futility. Violence creates many more social problems than it solves. And I've said, in so many instances, that as the Negro, in particular, and colored peoples all over the world struggle for freedom, if they succumb to the temptation of using violence in their struggle, unborn generations will be the recipients of a long and desolate night of bitterness, and our chief legacy to the future will be an endless reign of meaningless chaos. Violence isn't the way.

Another way is to acquiesce and to give in, to resign yourself to the oppression. Some people do that. They discover the difficulties of the wilderness moving into the promised land, and they would rather go back to the despots of Egypt because it's difficult to get in the promised land. And so they resign themselves to the fate of oppression; they somehow acquiesce to this thing. But that too isn't the way because non-cooperation with evil is as much a moral obligation as is cooperation with good.

But there is another way. And that is to organize mass nonviolent resistance based on the principle of love. It seems to me that this is the only way as our eyes look to the future. As we look out across the years and across the generations, let us develop and move right here. We must discover the power of love, the power, the redemptive power of love. And when we discover that, we will be able to make of this old world a new world. We will be able to make men better. Love is the only way. Jesus discovered that.

Not only did Jesus discover it, even great military leaders discover that. One day as Napoleon came toward the end of his career and looked back across the years—the great Napoleon that at a very early age had all but conquered the world. He was not stopped until he became, till he moved out to the battle of Leipzig and then to Waterloo. But that same Napoleon one day stood back and looked across the years, and said: "Alexander, Caesar, Charlemagne, and I have built great empires. But upon what did they depend? They depended upon force. But long ago Jesus started an empire that depended on love, and even to this day millions will die for him."

Yes, I can see Jesus walking around the hills and the valleys of Palestine. And I can see him looking out at the Roman Empire with all of her fascinating and intricate military machinery. But in the midst of that, I can hear him saying: "I will not use this method. Neither will I hate the Roman Empire."... *[Recording interrupted]*

And I'm proud to stand here in Dexter this morning and say that that army is still marching. It grew up from a group of eleven or twelve men to more than seven hundred million today. Because of the power and influence of the personality of this Christ, he was able to split history into A.D. and B.C. Because of his power, he was able to shake the hinges from the gates of the Roman Empire. And all around the world this morning, we can hear the glad echo of heaven ring:

> *Jesus shall reign wherever sun*
> *Does his successive journeys run;*
> *His kingdom spreads from shore to shore,*
> *Till moon shall wane and wax no more.*

We can hear another chorus singing: "All hail the power of Jesus' name!"

We can hear another chorus singing: "Hallelujah, hallelujah! He's King of Kings and Lord of Lords. Hallelujah, hallelujah!"

We can hear another choir singing:

In Christ there is no East or West.
In Him no North or South,
But one great Fellowship of Love
Throughout the whole wide world.

This is the only way.

And our civilization must discover that. Individuals must discover that as they deal with other individuals. There is a little tree planted on a little hill and on that tree hangs the most influential character that ever came in this world. But never feel that that tree is a meaningless drama that took place on the stages of history. Oh no, it is a telescope through which we look out into the long vista of eternity, and see the love of God breaking forth into time. It is an eternal reminder to a power-drunk generation that love is the only way. It is an eternal reminder to a generation depending on nuclear and atomic energy, a generation depending on physical violence, that love is the only creative, redemptive, transforming power in the universe.

So this morning, as I look into your eyes, and into the eyes of all of my brothers in Alabama and all over America and over the world, I say to you, "I love you. I would rather die than hate you." And I'm foolish enough to believe that through the power of this love somewhere, men of the most recalcitrant bent will be transformed. And then we will be in God's kingdom. We will be able to matriculate into the university of eternal life because we had the power to love our enemies, to bless those persons that cursed us, to even decide to be good to those persons who hated us, and we even prayed for those persons who despitefully used us.

Oh God, help us in our lives and in all of our attitudes to work out this controlling force of love, this controlling power that can solve every problem that we confront in all areas. Oh, we talk about politics; we talk about the problems facing our atomic civilization. Grant that all men will come together and discover that as we solve the crisis and solve these problems—the international problems, the problems of atomic energy, the problems of nuclear energy, and yes, even the race problem—let us join together in a great fellowship of love and bow down at the feet of Jesus. Give us this strong determination. In the name and spirit of this Christ, we pray. Amen.

Reflection Questions

1. Dr. King says that a crucial step in learning to love one's enemies is to "begin by analyzing yourself." Why is this a worthwhile but difficult task? What might we learn in this process of self-analysis that helps us to understand others?

2. Why might introspection and self-analysis be difficult—yet valuable—for our political leaders? What can be learned based on Dr. King's examples of communism and democracy?

3. Describe the difference between "isness" and "oughtness." Why is it important to recognize these two characteristics within ourselves? How does understanding these two ideas help us to understand our enemies?

4. Dr. King asserts that revenge and retaliation hurt whom ultimately? Conversely, what does he say about the redemptive power of love? How does love help, then, to make us whole?

A Knock at Midnight

This is another of the sermons that Dr. King included in *Strength to Love* (1963), a book that made his sermons available to readers of all races. In it, Dr. King criticizes Christians for often ignoring the needs of those who "knock on the door of the church," seeking "the bread of social justice" only to be "ignored or told to wait until later, which almost always means never." *Strength to Love* revealed Dr. King as a well-educated writer and religious leader who was willing to criticize religious hypocrisy, and whose ideas about human rights and social justice extended beyond the American civil rights movement.

> *Which of you who has a friend will go*
> *to him at midnight and say to him,*
> *"Friend, lend me three loaves; for a friend*
> *of mine has arrived on a journey, and*
> *I have nothing to set before him"?*

LUKE 11:5–6, RSV

Although this parable is concerned with the power of persistent prayer, it may also serve as a basis for our thought concerning many contemporary problems and the role of the church in

From Strength to Love *(New York: Harper & Row, 1963), reprinted in* A Gift of Love: Sermons from Strength to Love *and Other Preachings (Beacon Press, 2012).*

grappling with them. It is midnight in the parable; it is also midnight in our world, and the darkness is so deep that we can hardly see which way to turn.

I

It is midnight within the social order. On the international horizon nations are engaged in a colossal and bitter contest for supremacy. Two world wars have been fought within a generation, and the clouds of another war are dangerously low. Man now has atomic and nuclear weapons that could within seconds completely destroy the major cities of the world. Yet the arms race continues and nuclear tests still explode in the atmosphere, with the grim prospect that the very air we breathe will be poisoned by radioactive fallout. Will these circumstances and weapons bring the annihilation of the human race?

When confronted by midnight in the social order we have in the past turned to science for help. And little wonder! On so many occasions science has saved us. When we were in the midnight of physical limitation and material inconvenience, science lifted us to the bright morning of physical and material comfort. When we were in the midnight of crippling ignorance and superstition, science brought us to the daybreak of the free and open mind. When we were in the midnight of dread plagues and diseases, science, through surgery, sanitation, and the wonder drugs, ushered in the bright day of physical health, thereby prolonging our lives and making for greater security and physical well-being. How naturally we turn to science in a day when the problems of the world are so ghastly and ominous.

But alas! science cannot now rescue us, for even the scientist is lost in the terrible midnight of our age. Indeed, science gave us the very instruments that threaten to bring universal suicide. So modern man faces a dreary and frightening midnight in the social order.

This midnight in man's external collective life is paralleled by midnight in his internal individual life. It is midnight within the psychological order. Everywhere, paralyzing fears harrow people by day and haunt them by night. Deep clouds of anxiety and depression are suspended in our mental skies. More people are emotionally disturbed today than at any other time of human history. The psychopathic wards of our hospitals are crowded, and the most popular psychologists today are the psychoanalysts. Bestsellers in psychology are books such as *Man Against Himself, The Neurotic Personality of Our Times*, and *Modern Man in Search of a Soul.* Bestsellers in religion are such books as *Peace of Mind* and *Peace of Soul.* The popular clergyman preaches soothing sermons on "How to Be Happy" and "How to Relax." Some have been tempted to revise Jesus' command to read, "Go ye into all the world, keep your blood pressure down, and, lo, I will make you a well-adjusted personality." All of this is indicative that it is midnight within the inner lives of men and women.

It is also midnight within the moral order. At midnight colors lose their distinctiveness and become a sullen shade of grey. Moral principles have lost their distinctiveness. For modern man, absolute right and absolute wrong are a matter of what the majority is doing. Right and wrong are relative to likes and dislikes and the customs of a particular community. We have unconsciously applied Einstein's theory of relativity, which properly described the physical universe, to the moral and ethical realm.

Midnight is the hour when men desperately seek to obey the eleventh commandment, "Thou shalt not get caught." According to the ethic of midnight, the cardinal sin is to be caught and the cardinal virtue is to get by. It is all right to lie, but one must lie with real finesse. It is all right to steal, if one is so dignified that, if caught, the charge becomes embezzlement, not robbery. It is permissible even to hate, if one so dresses his hating in the garments of love that hating appears to be loving. The Darwinian concept of the survival of the fittest has been substituted by a philosophy of the survival of the slickest. This mentality has brought a tragic breakdown of moral standards, and the midnight of moral degeneration deepens.

II

As in the parable, so in our world today, the deep darkness of midnight is interrupted by the sound of a knock. On the door of the church millions of people knock. In this country the roll of church members is longer than ever before. More than one hundred and fifteen million people are at least paper members of some church or synagogue. This represents an increase of 100 percent since 1929, although the population has increased by only 31 percent.

Visitors to Soviet Russia, whose official policy is atheistic, report that the churches in that nation not only are crowded, but that attendance continues to grow. Harrison Salisbury, in an article in the *New York Times*, states that Communist officials are disturbed that so many young people express a growing interest in the church and religion. After forty years of the most vigorous efforts to suppress religion, the hierarchy of the Communist party now faces the inescapable fact that millions of people are knocking on the door of the church.

This numerical growth should not be overemphasized. We must not be tempted to confuse spiritual power and large numbers. Jumboism, as someone has called it, is an utterly fallacious standard for measuring positive power. An increase in quantity does not automatically bring an increase in quality. A larger membership does not necessarily represent a correspondingly increased commitment to Christ. Almost always the creative, dedicated minority has made the world better. But although a numerical growth in church membership does not necessarily reflect a concomitant increase in ethical commitment, millions of people do feel that the church provides an answer to the deep confusion that encompasses their lives. It is still the one familiar landmark where the weary traveler by midnight comes. It is the one house which stands where it has always stood, the house to which the man traveling at midnight either comes or refuses to come. Some decide not to come. But the many who come and knock are desperately seeking a little bread to tide them over.

The traveler asks for three loaves of bread. He wants the bread of faith. In a generation of so many colossal disappointments, men have lost faith in God, faith in man, and faith in the future. Many feel as did William Wilberforce, who in 1801 said, "I dare not marry—the future is so unsettled," or as did William Pitt, who in 1806 said, "There is scarcely anything 'round us but ruin and despair." In the midst of staggering disillusionment, many cry for the bread of faith.

There is also a deep longing for the bread of hope. In the early years of this century many people did not hunger for this bread. The days of the first telephones, automobiles, and airplanes gave them a radiant optimism. They worshiped at the shrine of inevitable progress. They believed that every new scientific achievement lifted man to higher levels of perfection. But then a series of tragic developments, revealing the selfishness and corruption of man, illustrated with frightening clarity the truth of Lord Acton's dictum, "Power tends to corrupt and absolute power corrupts absolutely." This awful discovery led to one of the most colossal breakdowns of optimism in history. For so many people, young and old, the light of hope went out, and they roamed wearily in the dark chambers of pessimism. Many concluded that life has no meaning. Some agreed with the philosopher Schopenhauer that life is an endless pain with a painful end, and that life is a tragicomedy played over and over again with only slight changes in costume and scenery. Others cried out with Shakespeare's Macbeth that life

> *Is a tale*
> *Told by an idiot, full of sound and fury,*
> *Signifying nothing.*

But even in the inevitable moments when all seems hopeless, men know that without hope they cannot really live, and in agonizing desperation they cry for the bread of hope.

And there is the deep longing for the bread of love. Everybody wishes to love and to be loved. He who feels that he is not loved feels that he does not count. Much has happened in the modern world to make men feel that they do not belong. Living in a world which has become oppressively impersonal, many of us have come to feel that we are little more than numbers. Ralph Borsodi, in an arresting picture of a world wherein numbers have replaced persons, writes that the modern mother is often maternity case No. 8434 and her child, after being fingerprinted and footprinted, becomes No. 8003, and that a funeral in a large city is an event in Parlor B with Class B flowers and decorations at which Preacher No. 14 officiates and Musician No. 84 sings Selection No. 174. Bewildered by this tendency to reduce man to a card in a vast index, man desperately searches for the bread of love.

III

When the man in the parable knocked on his friend's door and asked for the three loaves of bread, he received the impatient retort, "Do not bother me; the door is now shut, and my children are with me in bed; I cannot get up and give you anything." How often have men experienced a similar disappointment when at midnight they knock on the door of the church. Millions of Africans, patiently knocking on the door of the Christian church where they seek the bread of social justice, have either been altogether ignored or told to wait until later, which almost always means never. Millions of American Negroes, starving for the want of the bread of freedom, have knocked again and again on the door of so-called white churches, but they have usually been greeted by a cold indifference or a blatant hypocrisy. Even the white religious leaders, who have a heartfelt desire to open the door and provide the bread, are often more cautious than courageous and more prone to follow the expedient than the ethical path. One of the shameful tragedies of history is that the very institution which should remove man from the midnight of racial segregation participates in creating and perpetuating the midnight.

In the terrible midnight of war, men have knocked on the door of the church to ask for the bread of peace, but the church has often disappointed them. What more pathetically reveals the irrelevancy of the church in present-day world affairs than its witness regarding war? In a world gone mad with arms buildups, chauvinistic passions, and imperialistic exploitation, the church has either endorsed these activities or remained appallingly silent. During the last two world wars, national churches even functioned as the ready lackeys of the state, sprinkling holy water upon the battleships and joining the mighty armies in singing "Praise the Lord and pass the ammunition." A weary world, pleading desperately for peace, has often found the church morally sanctioning war.

And those who have gone to the church to seek the bread of economic justice have been left in the frustrating midnight of economic privation. In many instances the church has so aligned itself with the privileged classes and so defended the status quo that it has been unwilling to answer the knock at midnight. The Greek church in Russia allied itself with the status quo and became so inextricably bound to the despotic czarist regime that it became impossible to be rid of the corrupt political and social system without being rid of the church. Such is the fate of every ecclesiastical organization that allies itself with things as they are.

The church must be reminded that it is not the master or the servant of the state, but rather the conscience of the state. It must be the guide and the critic of the state, and never its tool. If the church does not recapture its prophetic zeal, it will become an irrelevant social club without moral or spiritual authority. If the church does not participate actively in the struggle for peace and for economic and racial justice, it will forfeit the loyalty of millions and cause men everywhere to say that it has atrophied its will. But if the church will free itself from the shackles of a deadening status quo, and, recovering its great historic mission, will speak and act fearlessly and insistently in terms of justice and peace, it will enkindle the imagination of mankind and fire the souls of men, imbuing them with a glowing and ardent love for truth, justice, and peace. Men far and near will know the church as a great fellowship of love that provides light and bread for lonely travelers at midnight.

While speaking of the laxity of the church, I must not overlook the fact that the so-called Negro church has also left men disappointed at midnight. I say so-called Negro church because ideally there can be no Negro or white church. It is to their everlasting shame that white Christians developed a system of racial segregation within the church, and inflicted so many indignities upon its Negro worshipers that they had to organize their own churches.

Two types of Negro churches have failed to provide bread. One burns with emotionalism, and the other freezes with classism. The former, reducing worship to entertainment, places more emphasis on volume than on content and confuses spirituality with muscularity. The danger in such a church is that the members may have more religion in their hands and feet than in their hearts and souls. At midnight this type of church has neither the vitality nor the relevant gospel to feed hungry souls.

The other type of Negro church that feeds no midnight traveler has developed a class system and boasts of its dignity, its membership of professional people, and its exclusiveness. In such a church the worship service is cold and meaningless, the music dull and uninspiring, and the sermon little more than a homily on current events. If the pastor says too much about Jesus Christ, the members feel that he is robbing the pulpit of dignity. If the choir sings a Negro spiritual, the members claim an affront to their class status. This type of church tragically fails to recognize that worship at its best is a social experience in which people from all levels of life come together to affirm their oneness and unity under God. At midnight men are altogether ignored because of their limited education, or they are given bread that has been hardened by the winter of morbid class consciousness.

IV

In the parable we notice that after the man's initial disappointment, he continued to knock on his friend's door. Because of his importunity— his persistence—he finally persuaded his friend to open the door. Many men continue to knock on the door of the church at midnight, even after the church has so bitterly disappointed them, because they know the bread of life is there. The church today is challenged to proclaim God's Son, Jesus Christ, to be the hope of men in all of their complex personal and social problems. Many will continue to come in quest of answers to life's problems. Many young people who knock on the door are perplexed by the uncertainties of life, confused by daily disappointments, and disillusioned by the ambiguities of history. Some who come have been taken from their schools and careers and cast in the role of soldiers. We must provide them with the fresh bread of hope and imbue them with the conviction that God has the power to bring good out of evil. Some who come are tortured by a nagging guilt resulting from their wandering in the midnight of ethical relativism and their surrender to the doctrine of self-expression. We must lead them to Christ who will offer them the fresh bread of forgiveness. Some who knock are tormented by the fear of death as they move toward the evening of life. We must provide them with the bread of faith in immortality, so that they may realize that this earthly life is merely an embryonic prelude to a new awakening.

Midnight is a confusing hour when it is difficult to be faithful. The most inspiring word that the church may speak is that no midnight long remains. The weary traveler by midnight who asks for bread is really seeking the dawn. Our eternal message of hope is that dawn will come. Our slave foreparents realized this. They were never unmindful of the fact of midnight, for always there was the rawhide whip of the overseer and the auction block where families were torn asunder to remind them of its reality. When they thought of the agonizing darkness of midnight, they sang:

> *Oh, nobody knows de trouble I've seen,*
> *Glory Hallelujah!*
> *Sometimes I'm up, sometimes I'm down,*
> *Oh, yes, Lord,*

Sometimes I'm almost to de groun',
Oh, yes, Lord,
Oh, nobody knows de trouble I've seen,
Glory Hallelujah!

Encompassed by a staggering midnight but believing that morning would come, they sang:

I'm so glad trouble don't last always.
O my Lord, O my Lord, what shall I do?

Their positive belief in the dawn was the growing edge of hope that kept the slaves faithful amid the most barren and tragic circumstances.

Faith in the dawn arises from the faith that God is good and just. When one believes this, he knows that the contradictions of life are neither final nor ultimate. He can walk through the dark night with the radiant conviction that all things work together for good for those that love God. Even the most starless midnight may herald the dawn of some great fulfillment.

At the beginning of the bus boycott in Montgomery, Alabama, we set up a voluntary car pool to get the people to and from their jobs. For eleven long months our car pool functioned extraordinarily well. Then Mayor Gayle introduced a resolution instructing the city's legal department to file such proceedings as it might deem proper to stop the operation of the car pool or any transportation system growing out of the bus boycott. A hearing was set for Tuesday, November 13, 1956.

At our regular weekly mass meeting, scheduled the night before the hearing, I had the responsibility of warning the people that the car pool would probably be enjoined. I knew that they had willingly suffered for nearly twelve months, but could we now ask them to walk back and forth to their jobs? And if not, would we be forced to admit that the protest had failed? For the first time I almost shrank from appearing before them.

When the evening came, I mustered sufficient courage to tell them the truth. I tried, however, to conclude on a note of hope. "We have moved all of these months," I said, "in the daring faith that God is with us in our struggle. The many experiences of days gone by have vindicated that faith in a marvelous way. Tonight we must believe that a way will be made out of no way." Yet I could feel the cold breeze of pessimism pass over the audience. The night was darker than a thousand midnights. The light of hope was about to fade and the lamp of faith to flicker.

A few hours later, before Judge Carter, the city argued that we were operating a "private enterprise" without a franchise. Our lawyers argued brilliantly that the car pool was a voluntary "share-a-ride" plan provided without profit as a service by Negro churches. It became obvious that Judge Carter would rule in favor of the city.

At noon, during a brief recess, I noticed an unusual commotion in the courtroom. Mayor Gayle was called to the back room. Several reporters moved excitedly in and out of the room. Momentarily a reporter came to the table where, as chief defendant, I sat with the lawyers. "Here is the decision that you have been waiting for," he said. "Read this release."

In anxiety and hope, I read these words: "The United States Supreme Court today unanimously ruled bus segregation unconstitutional in Montgomery, Alabama." My heart throbbed with an inexpressible joy. The darkest hour of our struggle had become the first hour of victory. Someone shouted from the back of the courtroom, "God Almighty has spoken from Washington!"

The dawn will come. Disappointment, sorrow, and despair are born at midnight, but morning follows. "Weeping may endure for a night," says the psalmist, "but joy cometh in the morning." This faith adjourns the assemblies of hopelessness and brings new light into the dark chambers of pessimism.

Reflection Questions

1. Why does Dr. King begin his sermon using such a bleak tone? What specific words create that tone? What is the significance of midnight as the time of day Dr. King selects?

2. What is the significance of the church and religion as a solution to midnight? In what ways has the church (of all races) failed those who knock at its doors? How must the church and religion combat issues that could overtake them (i.e., emotionalism and classism)?

3. How have people been disappointed by not having their knocks answered? Dr. King contends that people are hungry for different types of bread. What are those types, and what does each provide? Which of these types of bread is most important?

4. How do the beliefs in persistence, faith, and hope offer a solution to the darkness of midnight? What makes each of those concepts achievable?

Nonviolent
Resistance

The Sword That Heals

In this essay, Dr. King explains the rationale for the nonviolent direct action used in the Birmingham campaign of 1963. During this campaign, Dr. King and the Southern Christian Leadership Conference (SCLC) joined the Alabama Christian Movement for Human Rights (ACMHR) in sustained protests during Easter season—the second-biggest shopping season of the year—to end segregation by the city's merchants. Dr. King's incarceration in April of that year, as well as the involvement of more than a thousand African American children as protestors, prompted heated negotiations with white leaders. After his release from jail, Dr. King worked diligently to reach a compromise, and on May 10 allegedly desegregated lunch counters removed BLACKS ONLY signs and opened new employment opportunities for African Americans.

In the summer of 1963 a need and a time and a circumstance and the mood of a people came together. In order to understand the present Revolution, it is necessary to examine in more extensive detail the psychological and social conditions that produced it and the events that brought the philosophy and method of nonviolent direct action into the forefront of the struggle.

It is important to understand, first of all, that the Revolution is not indicative of a sudden loss of patience within the Negro. The Negro had

From Why We Can't Wait *(Harper & Row, 1963, 1964, reprinted by Beacon Press, 2010).*

never really been patient in the pure sense of the word. The posture of silent waiting was forced upon him psychologically because he was shackled physically.

In the days of slavery, this suppression was openly, scientifically and consistently applied. Sheer physical force kept the Negro captive at every point. He was prevented from learning to read and write, prevented by laws actually inscribed in the statute books. He was forbidden to associate with other Negroes living on the same plantation, except when weddings or funerals took place. Punishment for any form of resistance or complaint about his condition could range from mutilation to death. Families were torn apart, friends separated, cooperation to improve their condition carefully thwarted. Fathers and mothers were sold from their children and children were bargained away from their parents. Young girls were, in many cases, sold to become the breeders of fresh generations of slaves. The slaveholders of America had devised with almost scientific precision their systems for keeping the Negro defenseless, emotionally and physically.

With the ending of physical slavery after the Civil War, new devices were found to "keep the Negro in his place." It would take volumes to describe these methods, extending from birth in jim-crow hospitals through burial in jim-crow sections of cemeteries. They are too well known to require a catalogue here. Yet one of the revelations during the past few years is the fact that the straitjackets of race prejudice and discrimination do not wear only southern labels. The subtle, psychological technique of the North has approached in its ugliness and victimization of the Negro the outright terror and open brutality of the South. The result has been a demeanor that passed for patience in the eyes of the white man, but covered a powerful impatience in the heart of the Negro.

For years, in the South, the white segregationist has been saying the Negro was "satisfied." He has claimed "we get along beautifully with our Negroes because we understand them. We only have trouble when outside agitators come in and stir it up." Many expressed this point of view knowing that it was a lie of majestic proportions. Others believed they were speaking the truth. For corroboration, they would tell you: "Why, I talked to my cook and she said …" or, "I discussed this frankly with the colored boy who works for us and I told him to express himself freely. He said …"

White people in the South may never fully know the extent to which Negroes defended themselves and protected their jobs—and, in many cases, their lives—by perfecting an air of ignorance and agreement. In days gone by, no cook would have dared to tell her employer what he ought to know. She had to tell him what he wanted to hear. She knew that the penalty for speaking the truth could be loss of her job.

During the Montgomery bus boycott, a white family summoned their Negro cook and asked her if she supported the terrible things the Negroes were doing, boycotting buses and demanding jobs.

"Oh, no, ma'am, I won't have anything to do with that boycott thing," the cook said. "I am just going to stay away from the buses as long as that trouble is going on." No doubt she left a satisfied audience. But as she walked home from her job, on feet already weary from a full day's work, she walked proudly, knowing that she was marching with a movement that would bring into being nonsegregated bus travel in Montgomery.

Jailing the Negro was once as much of a threat as the loss of a job. To any Negro who displayed a spark of manhood, a southern law-enforcement officer could say: "Nigger, watch your step, or I'll put you in jail." The Negro knew what going to jail meant. It meant not only confinement and isolation from his loved ones. It meant that at the jailhouse he could probably expect a severe beating. And it meant that his day in court, if he had it, would be a mockery of justice.

Even today there still exists in the South—and in certain areas of the North—the license that our society allows to unjust officials who implement their authority in the name of justice to practice injustice against minorities. Where, in the days of slavery, social license and custom placed the unbridled power of the whip in the hands of overseers and masters, today—especially in the southern half of the nation—armies of officials are clothed in uniform, invested with authority, armed with the instruments of violence and death and conditioned to believe that they can intimidate, maim or kill Negroes with the same recklessness that once motivated the slaveowner. If one doubts this conclusion, let him search the records and find how rarely in any southern state a police officer has been punished for abusing a Negro.

Since nonviolent action has entered the scene, however, the white man has gasped at a new phenomenon. He has seen Negroes, by the hundreds and by the thousands, marching toward him, knowing they are going to jail, wanting to go to jail, willing to accept the confinement, willing to risk the beatings and the uncertain justice of the southern courts.

There were no more powerful moments in the Birmingham episode than during the closing days of the campaign, when Negro youngsters ran after white policemen, asking to be locked up. There was an element of unmalicious mischief in this. The Negro youngsters, although perfectly willing to submit to imprisonment, knew that we had already filled up the jails, and that the police had no place left to take them.

When, for decades, you have been able to make a man compromise his manhood by threatening him with a cruel and unjust punishment, and when suddenly he turns upon you and says: "Punish me. I do not deserve it. But because I do not deserve it, I will accept it so that the world will know that I am right and you are wrong," you hardly know what to do. You feel defeated and secretly ashamed. You know that this man is as good a man as you are; that from some mysterious source he has found the courage and the conviction to meet physical force with soul force.

So it was that, to the Negro, going to jail was no longer a disgrace but a badge of honor. The Revolution of the Negro not only attacked the external cause of his misery, but revealed him to himself. He was *somebody*. He had a sense of *somebodiness*. He was *impatient* to be free.

In the past decade, still another technique had begun to replace the old methods for thwarting the Negroes' dreams and aspirations. This is the method known as "tokenism." The dictionary interprets the word "token" in the following manner: "A symbol. Indication, evidence, as a token of friendship, a keepsake. A piece of metal used in place of a coin, as for paying carfare on conveyances operated by those who sell the tokens. A sign, a mark, emblem, memorial, omen."

When the Supreme Court modified its decision on school desegregation by approving the Pupil Placement Law, it permitted tokenism to corrupt its intent. It meant that Negroes could be handed the glitter of metal symbolizing the true coin, and authorizing a short-term trip toward democracy. But he who sells you the token instead of the coin always retains the power to revoke its worth, and to command you to get off the bus before you have reached your destination. Tokenism is a promise to pay. Democracy, in its finest sense, is payment.

The Negro wanted to feel pride in his race? With tokenism, the solution was simple. If all twenty million Negroes would keep looking at Ralph Bunche, the one man in so exalted a post would generate such a volume of pride that it could be cut into portions and served to everyone. A judge here and a judge there; an executive behind a polished desk in a carpeted office; a high government administrator with a toehold on a cabinet post; one student in a Mississippi university lofted there by an army; three Negro children admitted to the whole high-school system of a major city—all these were tokens used to obscure the persisting reality of segregation and discrimination.

For a decade the hard struggles had culminated in limited gains, which, if they advanced at all, crawled sluggishly forward. Schools, jobs, housing, voting rights and political positions—in each of these areas, manipulation with tokenism was the rule. Negroes had begun to feel that a policy was crystallizing, that all their struggles had brought them merely to a new level in which a selected few would become educated, honored and integrated to represent and substitute for the many.

Those who argue in favor of tokenism point out that we must begin somewhere; that it is unwise to spurn any breakthrough, no matter how limited. This position has a certain validity, and the Negro freedom movement has more often than not attained broad victories which had small beginnings. There is a critical distinction, however, between a modest start and tokenism. The tokenism Negroes condemn is recognizable because it is an end in itself. Its purpose is not to begin a process, but instead to end the process of protest and pressure. It is a hypocritical gesture, not a constructive first step.

I have gone into the Negro's resentment of tokenism at some length for I believe that analyzing his feelings about it will help to elucidate the uncompromising position he takes today. I think it will explain why he believes that half a loaf is no bread. I think it will justify his conviction that he must not turn back.

As I write, at the end of the first long season of Revolution, the Negro is not unmindful of or indifferent to the progress that has already been made. He notes with approval the radical change in the administration's approach to civil rights, and the small but visible gains being made on various fronts across the country. If he is still saying, "Not enough," it is because he does not feel that he should be expected to be *grateful* for the halting and inadequate attempts of his society to catch up with the basic rights he ought to have inherited automatically, centuries ago, by virtue of his membership in the human family and his American birthright.

In this conviction, he subscribes to the words of President Kennedy, uttered on June 11, 1963, only a few months before his tragic death: "We are confronted primarily with a moral issue. It is as old as the Scriptures and is as clear as the American Constitution. The heart of the question is whether all Americans are to be afforded equal rights and equal opportunities ... Those who do nothing are inviting shame as well as violence. Those who act boldly are recognizing right as well as reality."

II

For a hundred years since emancipation, Negroes had searched for the elusive path to freedom. They knew that they had to fashion a body of tactics suitable for their unique and special conditions. The words of the Constitution had declared them free, but life had told them that they were a twice-burdened people—they lived in the lowest stratum of society, and within it they were additionally imprisoned by a caste of color.

For decades the long and winding trails led to dead ends. Booker T. Washington, in the dark days that followed Reconstruction, advised them: "Let down your buckets where you are." Be content, he said in effect, with doing well what the times permit you to do at all. However, this path, they soon felt, had too little freedom in its present and too little promise in its future.

Dr. W. E. B. Du Bois, in his earlier years at the turn of the century, urged the "talented tenth" to rise and pull behind it the mass of the race. His doctrine served somewhat to counteract the apparent resignation of Booker T. Washington's philosophy. Yet, in the very nature of Du Bois's outlook there was no role for the whole people. It was a tactic for an aristocratic elite who would themselves be benefited while leaving behind the "untalented" 90 percent.

After the First World War, Marcus Garvey made an appeal to the race that had the virtue of rejecting concepts of inferiority. He called for a return to Africa and a resurgence of race pride. His movement attained mass dimensions, and released a powerful emotional response because it touched a truth which had long been dormant in the mind of the Negro. There was reason to be proud of their heritage as well as of their bitterly won achievements in America. Yet his plan was doomed because an exodus to Africa in the twentieth century by a people who had struck roots for three and a half centuries in the New World did not have the ring of progress.

With the death of the Garvey movement, the way opened for the development of the doctrine which held the center of the stage for almost thirty years. This was the doctrine, consistently championed and ably conducted by the National Association for the Advancement of Colored People, that placed its reliance on the Constitution and the federal law. Under this doctrine, it was felt that the federal courts were the vehicle that could be utilized to combat oppression, particularly in southern states, which were operating under the guise of legalistics to keep the Negro down.

Under brilliant and dedicated leadership, the N.A.A.C.P. moved relentlessly to win many victories in the courts. The most notable of these established the right of the Negro to participate in national elections, striking down evasive devices such as the "grandfather clause," white primaries and others. Beyond doubt, the doctrine of change through legal recourse reached flood tide in the education decisions. Yet the failure of the nation, over a decade, to implement the majestic implications of these decisions caused the slow ebb of the Negro's faith in litigation as the dominant method to achieve his freedom. In his eyes, the doctrine of legal change had become the doctrine of slow token change and, as a sole weapon of struggle, now proved its unsuitability. At the time of this growing realization, during the mid-fifties, Negroes were in the grip of a crisis. Their movement no longer had a promising basic doctrine, a detailed and charted course pointing the way to their freedom.

It is an axiom of social change that no revolution can take place without a methodology suited to the circumstances of the period. During the fifties many voices offered substitutes for the tactic of legal recourse. Some called for a colossal blood bath to cleanse the nation's ills. To support their advocacy of violence and its incitement, they pointed to an historical tradition reaching back from the American Civil War to Spartacus in Rome. But the Negro in the South in 1955, assessing the power of the forces arrayed against him, could not perceive the slightest prospect of victory in this approach. He was unarmed, unorganized, untrained, disunited and, most important, psychologically and morally unprepared for the deliberate spilling of blood. Although his desperation had prepared him with the courage to die for freedom if necessary, he was not willing to commit himself to racial suicide with no prospect of victory.

Perhaps even more vital in the Negro's resistance to violence was the force of his deeply rooted spiritual beliefs. In Montgomery, after a courageous woman, Rosa Parks, had refused to move to the back of the bus, and so began the revolt that led to the boycott of 1955–56, the Negro's developing campaign against that city's racial injustice was based in the churches of the community. Throughout the South, for some years prior to Montgomery, the Negro church had emerged with increasing impact in the civil-rights struggle. Negro ministers, with a growing awareness that the true witness of a Christian life is the projection of a social gospel, had accepted leadership in the fight for racial justice, had played important roles in a number of N.A.A.C.P. groups, and were making their influence felt throughout the freedom movement.

The doctrine they preached was a nonviolent doctrine. It was not a doctrine that made their followers yearn for revenge but one that called upon them to champion change. It was not a doctrine that asked an eye for an eye but one that summoned men to seek to open the eyes of blind prejudice. The Negro turned his back on force not only because he knew he could not win his freedom through physical force but also because he believed that through physical force he could lose his soul.

There were echoes of Marcus Garvey in another solution proffered the Negro during this period of crisis and change. The Black Muslims, convinced that an interracial society promised nothing but tragedy and frustration for the Negro, began to urge a permanent separation of the races. Unlike Garvey's prescription, the Muslims appeared to believe the separation could be achieved in this country without a long sea voyage to Africa, but their message resembled Garvey's in another respect: It won only fractional support from the Negro community. Most of those to whom the Muslims appealed were in fact expressing resentment for the lack of militancy which had long prevailed in the freedom movement. When the Negroes' fighting spirit soared in the summer of 1963, the appeal of the Muslims declined precipitously. Today, as I travel throughout the country, I am struck by how few American Negroes (except in a handful of big-city ghettos) have even heard of the Muslim movement, much less given allegiance to its pessimistic doctrine.

Yet another tactic was offered the Negro. He was encouraged to seek unity with the millions of disadvantaged whites of the South, whose

basic need for social change paralleled his own. Theoretically, this pro-
posal held a measure of logic, for it is undeniable that great masses of
southern whites exist in conditions scarcely better than those which af-
flict the Negro. But the rationale of this theory wilted under the heat of
fact. The need for immediate change was more urgently felt and more
bitterly realized by the Negro than by the exploited white. As individuals, the whites could better their situation without the barrier that
society places in front of a man whose racial identification by color is inescapable. Moreover, the underprivileged southern whites saw the color
that separated them from Negroes more clearly than they saw the circumstances that bound them together in mutual interest. Negroes were
therefore forced to face the fact that, in the South, they must move without allies; and yet the coiled power of state force made such a prospect
appear both futile and quixotic.

III

Fortunately, history does not pose problems without eventually produc-
ing solutions. The disenchanted, the disadvantaged and the disinherited
seem, at times of deep crisis, to summon up some sort of genius that
enables them to perceive and capture the appropriate weapons to carve
out their destiny. Such was the peaceable weapon of nonviolent direct
action, which materialized almost overnight to inspire the Negro, and
was seized in his outstretched hands with a powerful grip.

Nonviolent action, the Negro saw, was the way to supplement—not
replace—the process of change through legal recourse. It was the way to
divest himself of passivity without arraying himself in vindictive force.
Acting in concert with fellow Negroes to assert himself as a citizen, he
would embark on a militant program to demand the rights which were
his: in the streets, on the buses, in the stores, the parks and other public
facilities.

The religious tradition of the Negro had shown him that the nonviolent resistance of the early Christians had constituted a moral offensive

of such overriding power that it shook the Roman Empire. American history had taught him that nonviolence in the form of boycotts and protests had confounded the British monarchy and laid the basis for freeing the colonies from unjust domination. Within his own century, the nonviolent ethic of Mahatma Gandhi and his followers had muzzled the guns of the British Empire in India and freed more than three hundred and fifty million people from colonialism.

Like his predecessors, the Negro was willing to risk martyrdom in order to move and stir the social conscience of his community and the nation. Instead of submitting to surreptitious cruelty in thousands of dark jail cells and on countless shadowed street corners, he would force his oppressor to commit his brutality openly—in the light of day—with the rest of the world looking on.

Acceptance of nonviolent direct action was a proof of a certain sophistication on the part of the Negro masses; for it showed that they dared to break with the old, ingrained concepts of our society. The eye-for-an-eye philosophy, the impulse to defend oneself when attacked, has always been held as the highest measure of American manhood. We are a nation that worships the frontier tradition, and our heroes are those who champion justice through violent retaliation against injustice. It is not simple to adopt the credo that moral force has as much strength and virtue as the capacity to return a physical blow; or that to refrain from hitting back requires more will and bravery than the automatic reflexes of defense.

Yet there is something in the American ethos that responds to the strength of moral force. I am reminded of the popular and widely respected novel and film *To Kill a Mockingbird*. Atticus Finch, a white southern lawyer, confronts a group of his neighbors who have become a lynch-crazed mob, seeking the life of his Negro client. Finch, armed with nothing more lethal than a lawbook, disperses the mob with the force of his moral courage, aided by his small daughter, who, innocently calling the would-be lynchers by name, reminds them that they are individual men, not a pack of beasts.

To the Negro in 1963, as to Atticus Finch, it had become obvious that nonviolence could symbolize the gold badge of heroism rather than the white feather of cowardice. In addition to being consistent with his religious precepts, it served his need to act on his own for his own liberation. It enabled him to transmute hatred into constructive energy, to seek not only to free himself but to free his oppressor from his sins. This transformation, in turn, had the marvelous effect of changing the face of the enemy. The enemy the Negro faced became not the individual who had oppressed him but the evil system which permitted that individual to do so.

The argument that nonviolence is a coward's refuge lost its force as its heroic and often perilous acts uttered their wordless but convincing rebuttal in Montgomery, in the sit-ins, on the freedom rides, and finally in Birmingham.

There is a powerful motivation when a suppressed people enlist in an army that marches under the banner of nonviolence. A nonviolent army has a magnificent universal quality. To join an army that trains its adherents in the methods of violence, you must be of a certain age. But in Birmingham, some of the most valued foot soldiers were youngsters ranging from elementary pupils to teenage high school and college students. For acceptance in the armies that maim and kill, one must be physically sound, possessed of straight limbs and accurate vision. But in Birmingham, the lame and the halt and the crippled could and did join up. Al Hibbler, the sightless singer, would never have been accepted in the United States Army or the army of any other nation, but he held a commanding position in our ranks.

In armies of violence, there is a caste of rank. In Birmingham, outside of the few generals and lieutenants who necessarily directed and coordinated operations, the regiments of the demonstrators marched in democratic phalanx. Doctors marched with window cleaners. Lawyers demonstrated with laundresses. PhD's and no-D's were treated with perfect equality by the registrars of the nonviolence movement.

As the broadcasting profession will confirm, no shows are so successful as those which allow for audience participation. In order to be some-body, people must feel themselves part of something. In the nonviolent army, there is room for everyone who wants to join up. There is no color distinction. There is no examination, no pledge, except that, as a soldier in the armies of violence is expected to inspect his carbine and keep it clean, nonviolent soldiers are called upon to examine and burnish their greatest weapons—their heart, their conscience, their courage and their sense of justice.

Nonviolent resistance paralyzed and confused the power structures against which it was directed. The brutality with which officials would have quelled the black individual became impotent when it could not be pursued with stealth and remain unobserved. It was caught—as a fugi-tive from a penitentiary is often caught—in gigantic circling spotlights. It was imprisoned in a luminous glare revealing the naked truth to the whole world. It is true that some demonstrators suffered violence, and that a few paid the extreme penalty of death. They were the martyrs of last summer who laid down their lives to put an end to the brutaliz-ing of thousands who had been beaten and bruised and killed in dark streets and back rooms of sheriffs' offices, day in and day out, in hun-dreds of summers past.

The striking thing about the nonviolent crusade of 1963 was that so few felt the sting of bullets or the clubbing of billies and nightsticks. Looking back, it becomes obvious that the oppressors were restrained not only because the world was looking but also because, standing before them, were hundreds, sometimes thousands, of Negroes who for the first time dared to look back at a white man, eye to eye. Whether through a decision to exercise wise restraint or the operation of a guilty conscience, many a hand was stayed on a police club and many a fire hose was restrained from vomiting forth its pressure. That the Revolu-tion was a comparatively bloodless one is explained by the fact that the Negro did not merely give lip service to nonviolence. The tactics the movement utilized, and that guided far-flung actions in cities dotted across the map, discouraged violence because one side would not resort to it and the other was so often immobilized by confusion, uncertainty and disunity.

Nonviolence had tremendous psychological importance to the Negro. He had to win and to vindicate his dignity in order to merit and enjoy his self-esteem. He had to let white men know that the picture of him as a clown—irresponsible, resigned and believing in his own inferiority—was a stereotype with no validity. This method was grasped by the Negro masses because it embodied the dignity of struggle, of moral conviction and self-sacrifice. The Negro was able to face his adversary, to concede to him a physical advantage and to defeat him because the superior force of the oppressor had become powerless.

To measure what this meant to the Negro may not be easy. But I am convinced that the courage and discipline with which Negro thousands accepted nonviolence healed the internal wounds of Negro millions who did not themselves march in the streets or sit in the jails of the South. One need not participate directly in order to be involved. For Negroes all over this nation, to identify with the movement, to have pride in those who were the principals, and to give moral, financial or spiritual support were to restore to them some of the pride and honor which had been stripped from them over the centuries.

IV

In the light of last summer's successful crusade, one might ask why it took the Negro eight years to apply the lessons of the Montgomery boycott to the problems of Birmingham, and the nation's other Birminghams, north and south.

A methodology and philosophy of revolution is neither born nor accepted overnight. From the moment it emerges, it is subjected to rigorous tests, opposition, scorn and prejudice. The old guard in any society resents new methods, for old guards wear the decorations and medals won by waging battle in the accepted manner. Often opposition comes not only from the conservatives, who cling to tradition, but also from the extremist militants, who favor neither the old nor the new.

Many of these extremists misread the significance and intent of nonviolence because they failed to perceive that militancy is also the father of the nonviolent way. Angry exhortation from street corners and stirring calls for the Negro to arm and go forth to do battle stimulate loud applause. But when the applause dies, the stirred and the stirring return to their homes, and lie in their beds for still one more night with no progress in view. They cannot solve the problem they face because they have offered no challenge but only a call to arms, which they themselves are unwilling to lead, knowing that doom would be its reward. They cannot solve the problem because they seek to overcome a negative situation with negative means. They cannot solve the problem because they do not reach and move into sustained action the large groups of people necessary to attract attention and convey the determination of the majority. The conservatives who say, "Let us not move so fast," and the extremists who say, "Let us go out and whip the world," would tell you that they are as far apart as the poles. But there is a striking parallel: They accomplish nothing; for they do not reach the people who have a crying need to be free.

One factor that helps to explain why the Negro nationally did not embrace the nonviolent ethic, immediately after Montgomery, was a fallacious and dangerously divisive philosophy spread by those who were either dishonest or ignorant. This philosophy held that nonviolent, direct action was a *substitute* for all other approaches, attacking especially the legal methods that up to the mid-fifties had brought such important, decisive court rulings and laws into being. The best way to defeat an army is to divide it. Negroes as well as whites have compounded confusion and distorted reality by defending the legal approach and condemning direct action, or defending direct action and condemning the legal approach.

Direct action is not a substitute for work in the courts and the halls of government. Bringing about passage of a new and broad law by a city council, state legislature or the Congress, or pleading cases before the courts of the land, does not eliminate the necessity for bringing about the mass dramatization of injustice in front of a city hall. Indeed, direct action and legal action complement one another; when skillfully employed, each becomes more effective.

The chronology of the sit-ins confirms this observation. Spontaneously born, but guided by the theory of nonviolent resistance, the lunch-counter sit-ins accomplished integration in hundreds of communities at the swiftest rate of change in the civil-rights movement up to that time. Yet, many communities successfully resisted lunch-counter desegregation, and pressed charges against the demonstrators. It was correct and effective that demonstrators should fill the jails; but it was necessary that these foot soldiers for freedom not be deserted to languish there or to pay excessive penalties for their devotion. Indeed, by creative use of the law, it was possible to prove that officials combating the demonstrations were using the power of the police state to deny the Negro equal protection under the law. This brought many of the cases squarely under the jurisdiction of the Fourteenth Amendment. As a consequence of combining direct and legal action, far-reaching precedents were established, which served, in turn, to extend the areas of desegregation.

Another reason for the delay in applying the lessons of Montgomery was the feeling abroad in the land that the success of the bus boycott was an isolated phenomenon, and that the Negro elsewhere would never be willing to sacrifice in such extreme measure. When, in Albany, Georgia, in 1962, months of demonstrations and jailings failed to accomplish the goals of the movement, reports in the press and elsewhere pronounced nonviolent resistance a dead issue.

There were weaknesses in Albany, and a share of the responsibility belongs to each of us who participated. However, none of us was so immodest as to feel himself master of the new theory. Each of us expected that setbacks would be a part of the ongoing effort. There is no tactical theory so neat that a revolutionary struggle for a share of power can be won merely by pressing a row of buttons. Human beings with all their faults and strengths constitute the mechanism of a social movement. They must make mistakes and learn from them, make more mistakes and learn anew. They must taste defeat as well as success, and discover how to live with each. Time and action are the teachers.

When we planned our strategy for Birmingham months later, we spent many hours assessing Albany and trying to learn from its errors. Our appraisals not only helped to make our subsequent tactics more effective, but revealed that Albany was far from an unqualified failure. Though lunch counters remained segregated, thousands of Negroes were added to the voting-registration rolls. In the gubernatorial elections that followed our summer there, a moderate candidate confronted a rabid segregationist. By reason of the expanded Negro vote, the moderate defeated the segregationist in the city of Albany, which in turn contributed to his victory in the state. As a result, Georgia elected its first governor pledged to respect and enforce the law equally.

Our movement had been checked in Albany but not defeated. City authorities had been obliged to close down facilities such as parks, libraries and bus lines to avoid integration. The authorities were crippling themselves, denying facilities to the white population in order to obstruct our progress. Someone observed that Samuel Johnson had called parks "the lungs of a city," and that Albany would have to breathe again even though the air, too, be desegregated.

Even had nonviolent resistance been soundly defeated in Albany, the alacrity with which the bells were tolled for it must arouse suspicion. The prompt interment of the theory was not a judicious conclusion but an attack. Albany, in fact, had proved how extraordinary was the Negro response to the appeal of nonviolence. Approximately 5 percent of the total Negro population went willingly to jail. Were that percentage duplicated in New York City, some fifty thousand Negroes would overflow its prisons. If a people can produce from its ranks 5 percent who will go voluntarily to jail for a just cause, surely nothing can thwart its ultimate triumph.

If, however, the detractors of nonviolence fell into error by magnifying temporary setbacks into catastrophic defeat, the adherents of the new theory must avoid exaggerating its powers. When we speak of filling the jails, we are talking of a tactic to be flexibly applied. No responsible person would promise to fill all jails everywhere at any time. Leaders indulge in bombast if they do not take all circumstances into account before calling upon their people to make a maximum sacrifice. Filling jails means that thousands of people must leave their jobs, perhaps to lose them, put off responsibilities, undergo harrowing psychological experiences for which law-abiding people are not routinely prepared. The miracle of nonviolence lies in the degree to which people will sacrifice under its inspiration, when the call is based on judgment.

Negroes are human, not superhuman. Like all people, they have differing personalities, diverse financial interests and varied aspirations. There are Negroes who will never fight for freedom. There are Negroes who will seek profit for themselves alone from the struggle. There are even some Negroes who will cooperate with their oppressors. These facts should distress no one. Every minority and every people has its share of opportunists, profiteers, freeloaders and escapists. The hammer blows of discrimination, poverty and segregation must warp and corrupt some. No one can pretend that because a people may be oppressed, every individual member is virtuous and worthy. The real issue is whether in the great mass the dominant characteristics are decency, honor and courage.

In 1963, once again life was proof that Negroes had their heroes, their masses of decent people, along with their lost souls. The doubts that millions had felt as to the efficacy of the nonviolent way were dissolved. And the Negro saw that by proving the sweeping and majestic power of nonviolence to bring about the beloved community, it might be possible for him to set an example to a whole world caught up in conflict.

V

In the entire country there was no place to compare with Birmingham. The largest industrial city in the South, Birmingham had become, in the thirties, a symbol for bloodshed when trade unions sought to organize. It was a community in which human rights had been trampled for so long that fear and oppression were as thick in its atmosphere as the smog from its factories. Its financial interests were interlocked with a power structure which spread throughout the South and radiated into the North.

The challenge to nonviolent, direct action could not have been staged in a more appropriate arena. In the summer of 1963, an army brandishing only the healing sword of nonviolence humbled the most powerful, the most experienced and the most implacable segregationists in the country. Birmingham was to emerge with a delicately poised peace, but without awaiting its implementation the Negro seized the weapon that had won that dangerous peace and swept across the land with it.

The victory of the theory of nonviolent direct action was a fact. Faith in this method had come to maturity in Birmingham. As a result, the whole spectrum of the civil-rights struggle would undergo basic change. Nonviolence had passed the test of its steel in the fires of turmoil. The united power of southern segregation was the hammer. Birmingham was the anvil.

Reflection Questions

1. Dr. King describes nonviolence as a response by African Americans to being "shackled physically." What were some of those ways? How were both the South and the North involved in maintaining those shackles?

2. How exactly did nonviolent resistance come to symbolize heroism rather than cowardice? What were some of the broad benefits of this approach to the many involved? What do those benefits suggest about the nature of an inclusive movement?

3. Dr. King recounts several attempts to end the oppression of African Americans that preceded nonviolent resistance. In those attempts, why was nonviolence the better solution? Be sure to draw on history and factual evidence to make your case.

4. What does Dr. King think about the tactic of nonviolent resistance versus that of using legal methods to work to pass new laws and change old ones? How do these two tactics help or hinder each other?

My Trip to the Land of Gandhi

In February 1959, two years after the successful conclusion of the Montgomery bus boycott, Dr. King, accompanied by his wife, Coretta, and historian Lawrence Reddick, traveled to India for a five-week tour. Dr. King's entourage was warmly welcomed by Indian political leaders and Gandhian activists. The visit deepened Dr. King's understanding of Gandhian principles, prompting him to call Gandhi "the guiding light of our technique of nonviolent social change" and to draw parallels between caste discrimination in India and racial discrimination in the United States.

For a long time I had wanted to take a trip to India. Even as a child the entire Orient held a strange fascination for me—the elephants, the tigers, the temples, the snake charmers and all the other storybook characters.

While the Montgomery boycott was going on, India's Gandhi was the guiding light of our technique of non-violent social change. We spoke of him often. So as soon as our victory over bus segregation was won, some of my friends said: "Why don't you go to India and see for yourself what the Mahatma, whom you so admire, has wrought."

In 1956 when Pandit Jawaharlal Nehru, India's Prime Minister, made a short visit to the United States, he was gracious enough to say that he wished that he and I had met and had his diplomatic representatives

Originally published in Ebony *(July 1959). This version published in* "A Single Garment of Destiny": A Global Vision of Justice *(Boston: Beacon Press, 2012).*

make inquiries as to the possibility of my visiting his country some time soon. Our former American ambassador to India, Chester Bowles, wrote me along the same lines.

But every time that I was about to make the trip, something would interfere. At one time it was my visit by prior commitment to Ghana. At another time my publishers were pressing me to finish writing *Stride Toward Freedom*. Then along came Mrs. Izola Ware Curry. When she struck me with that Japanese letter opener on that Saturday afternoon in September as I sat autographing books in a Harlem store, she not only knocked out the travel plans that I had but almost everything else as well.

After I recovered from this near-fatal encounter and was finally released by my doctors, it occurred to me that it might be better to get in the trip to India before plunging too deeply once again into the sea of the Southern segregation struggle.

I preferred not to take this long trip alone and asked my wife and my friend, Lawrence Reddick, to accompany me. Coretta was particularly interested in the women of India and Dr. Reddick in the history and government of that great country. He had written my biography, *Crusader Without Violence*, and said that my true test would come when the people who knew Gandhi looked me over and passed judgment upon me and the Montgomery movement. The three of us made up a sort of 3-headed team with six eyes and six ears for looking and listening.

The Christopher Reynolds Foundation made a grant through the American Friends Service Committee to cover most of the expenses of the trip and the Southern Christian Leadership Conference and the Montgomery Improvement Association added their support. The Gandhi Memorial Trust of India extended an official invitation, through diplomatic channels, for our visit.

And so on February 3, 1959, just before midnight, we left New York by plane. En route we stopped in Paris with Richard Wright, an old friend of Reddick's, who brought us up to date on European attitudes on the Negro question and gave us a taste of the best French cooking.

We missed our plane connection in Switzerland because of fog, arriving in India after a roundabout route, two days late. But from the time we came down out of the clouds at Bombay on February 10, until March 10, when we waved goodbye at the New Delhi airport, we had one of the [most] concentrated and eye-opening experiences of our lives. There is so much to tell that I can only touch upon a few of the high points.

At the outset, let me say that we had a grand reception in India. The people showered upon us the most generous hospitality imaginable. We were graciously received by the Prime Minister, the President and the Vice-President of the nation; members of Parliament, Governors and Chief Ministers of various Indian states; writers, professors, social reformers and at least one saint. Since our pictures were in the newspapers very often it was not unusual for us to be recognized by crowds in public places and on public conveyances. Occasionally I would take a morning walk in the large cities, and out of the most unexpected places someone would emerge and ask: "Are you Martin Luther King?"

Virtually every door was open to us. We had hundreds of invitations that the limited time did not allow us to accept. We were looked upon as brothers with the color of our skins as something of an asset. But the strongest bond of fraternity was the common cause of minority and colonial peoples in America, Africa and Asia struggling to throw off racialism and imperialism.

We had the opportunity to share our views with thousands of Indian people through endless conversations and numerous discussion sessions. I spoke before university groups and public meetings all over India. Because of the keen interest that the Indian people have in the race problem these meetings were usually packed. Occasionally interpreters were used, but on the whole I spoke to audiences that understood English.

The Indian people love to listen to the Negro spirituals. Therefore, Coretta ended up singing as much as I lectured. We discovered that autograph seekers are not confined to America. After appearances in public meetings and while visiting villages we were often besieged for autographs. Even while riding planes, more than once pilots came into the cabin from the cockpit requesting our signatures.

We got a good press throughout our stay. Thanks to the Indian papers, the Montgomery bus boycott was already well known in that country. Indian publications perhaps gave a better continuity of our 381-day bus strike than did most of our papers in the United States. Occasionally I meet some American fellow citizen who even now asks me how the bus boycott is going, apparently never having read that our great day of bus integration, December 21, 1956, closed that chapter of our history.

We held press conferences in all of the larger cities—Delhi, Calcutta, Madras and Bombay—and talked with newspaper men almost everywhere we went. They asked sharp questions and at times appeared to be hostile but that was just their way of bringing out the story that they were after. As reporters, they were scrupulously fair with us and in their editorials showed an amazing grasp of what was going on in America and other parts of the world.

The trip had a great impact upon me personally. It was wonderful to be in Gandhi's land, to talk with his son, his grandsons, his cousin and other relatives; to share the reminiscences of his close comrades; to visit his ashrama, to see the countless memorials for him and finally to lay a wreath on his entombed ashes at Rajghat. I left India more convinced than ever before that non-violent resistance is the most potent weapon available to oppressed people in their struggle for freedom. It was a marvelous thing to see the amazing results of a non-violent campaign. The aftermath of hatred and bitterness that usually follows a violent campaign was found nowhere in India. Today a mutual friendship based on complete equality exists between the Indian and British people within the commonwealth. The way of acquiescence leads to moral and spiritual suicide. The way of violence leads to bitterness in the survivors and brutality in the destroyers. But, the way of non-violence leads to redemption and the creation of the beloved community.

The spirit of Gandhi is very much alive in India today. Some of his disciples have misgivings about this when they remember the drama of the fight for national independence and when they look around and find nobody today who comes near the stature of the Mahatma. But any objective observer must report that Gandhi is not only the greatest figure in India's history but that his influence is felt in almost every aspect of life and public policy today.

India can never forget Gandhi. For example, the Gandhi Memorial Trust (also known as the Gandhi Smarak Nidhi) collected some $130 million soon after the death of "the father of the nation." This was perhaps the largest, spontaneous, mass monetary contribution to the memory of a single individual in the history of the world. This fund, along with support from the Government and other institutions, is resulting in the spread and development of Gandhian philosophy, the implementing of his constructive program, the erection of libraries and the publication of works by and about the life and times of Gandhi. Posterity could not escape him even if it tried. By all standards of measurement, he is one of the half dozen greatest men in world history.

I was delighted that the Gandhians accepted us with open arms. They praised our experiment with the non-violent resistance technique at Montgomery. They seem to look upon it as an outstanding example of the possibilities of its use in western civilization. To them as to me it also suggests that non-violent resistance *when planned and positive in action* can work effectively even under totalitarian regimes.

We argued this point at some length with the groups of African students who are today studying in India. They felt that non-violent resistance could only work in a situation where the resisters had a potential ally in the conscience of the opponent. We soon discovered that they, like many others, tended to confuse passive resistance with non-resistance. This is completely wrong. True non-violent resistance is not unrealistic submission to evil power. It is rather a courageous confrontation of evil by the power of love, in the faith that it is better to be the recipient of violence than the inflictor of it, since the latter only multiplies the existence of violence and bitterness in the universe, while the former may develop a sense of shame in the opponent, and thereby bring about a transformation and change of heart.

Non-violent resistance does call for love, but it is not a sentimental love. It is a very stern love that would organize itself into collective action to right a wrong by taking on itself suffering. While I understand the reasons why oppressed people often turn to violence in their struggle for freedom, it is my firm belief that the crusade for independence and human dignity that is now reaching a climax in Africa will have a more positive effect on the world, if it is waged along the lines that were first demonstrated in that continent by Gandhi himself.

India is a vast country with vast problems. We flew over the long stretches, from North to South, East to West; took trains for shorter jumps and used automobiles and jeeps to get us into the less accessible places.

India is about a third the size of the United States but has almost three times as many people. Everywhere we went we saw crowded humanity— on the roads, in the city streets and squares, even in the villages.

Most of the people are poor and poorly dressed. The average income per person is less than $70 per year. Nevertheless, their turbans for their heads, loose flowing, wrap-around *dhotis* that they wear instead of trousers and the flowing saris that the women wear instead of dresses are colorful and picturesque. Many Indians wear part native and part western dress.

We think that we in the United States have a big housing problem but in the city of Bombay, for example, over a half million people sleep out of doors every night. These are mostly unattached, unemployed or partially employed males. They carry their bedding with them like foot soldiers and unroll it each night in any unoccupied space they can find—on the sidewalk, in a railroad station or at the entrance of a shop that is closed for the evening.

The food shortage is so widespread that it is estimated that less than thirty percent of the people get what we would call three square meals a day. During our great depression of the 1930's, we spoke of "a third of a nation" being "ill-housed, ill clad and ill fed." For India today, simply change one third to two thirds in that statement and that would make it about right.

As great as is unemployment, under-employment is even greater. Seventy percent of the Indian people are classified as agricultural workers and most of these do less than 200 days of farm labor per year because of the seasonal fluctuations and other uncertainties of mother nature. Jobless men roam the city streets.

Great ills flow from the poverty of India but strangely there is relatively little crime. Here is another concrete manifestation of the wonderful spiritual quality of the Indian people. They are poor, jammed together and half starved but they do not take it out on each other. They are a kindly people. They do not abuse each other—verbally or physically—as readily as we do. We saw but one fist fight in India during our stay.

In contrast to the poverty-stricken, there are Indians who are rich, have luxurious homes, landed estates, fine clothes and show evidence of over-eating. The bourgeoise [sic]—white, black or brown—behaves about the same the world over.

And then there is, even here, the problem of segregation. We call it race in America; they call it caste in India. In both places it means that some are considered inferior, treated as though they deserve less.

We were surprised and delighted to see that India has made greater progress in the fight against caste "untouchability" than we have made here in our own country against race segregation. Both nations have federal laws against discrimination (acknowledging, of course, that the decision of our Supreme Court is the law of our land). But after this has been said, we must recognize that there are great differences between what India has done and what we have done on a problem that is very similar. The leaders of India have placed their moral power behind their law. From the Prime Minister down to the village councilmen, everybody declares publicly that untouchability is wrong. But in the United States some of our highest officials decline to render a moral judgment on segregation and some from the South publicly boast of their determination to maintain segregation. This would be unthinkable in India.

Moreover, Gandhi not only spoke against the caste system but he acted against it. He took "untouchables" by the hand and led them into the temples from which they had been excluded. To equal that, President Eisenhower would take a Negro child by the hand and lead her into Central High School in Little Rock.

Gandhi also renamed the untouchables, calling them "Harijans," which means "children of God."

The government has thrown its full weight behind the program of giving the Harijans an equal chance in society—especially when it comes to job opportunities, education and housing.

India's leaders, in and out of government, are conscious of their country's other great problems and are heroically grappling with them. The country seems to be divided. Some say that India should become westernized and modernized as quickly as possible so that she might raise her standards of living. Foreign capital and foreign industry should be invited in, for in this lies the salvation of the almost desperate situation.

On the other hand, there are others—perhaps the majority—who say that westernization will bring with it the evils of materialism, cut throat competition and rugged individualism; that India will lose her soul if she takes to chasing Yankee dollars; and that the big machine will only raise the living standards of the comparative few workers who get jobs but that the greater number of people will be displaced and will thus be worse off than they are now.

Prime Minister Nehru, who is at once an intellectual and a man charged with the practical responsibility of heading the government, seems to steer a middle course between these extreme attitudes. In our talk with him he indicated that he felt that some industrialization was absolutely necessary; that there were some things that only big or heavy industry could do for the country but that if the state keeps a watchful eye on the developments, most of the pitfalls may be avoided.

At the same time, Mr. Nehru gives support to the movement that would encourage and expand the handicraft arts such as spinning and weaving in home and village and thus leaving as much economic self help and autonomy as possible to the local community.

There is a great movement in India that is almost unknown in America. At its center is the campaign for land reform known as Bhoodan. It would solve India's great economic and social change by consent, not by force. The Bhoodanists are led by the sainted Vinoba Bhave and Jayaprakash Narayan, a highly sensitive intellectual who was trained in American colleges. Their ideal is the self-sufficient village. Their program envisions

1. *Persuading* large land owners to give up some of their holding to landless peasants;

2. *Persuading* small land owners to give up their individual ownership for common cooperative ownership by the villages;

3. *Encouraging* farmers and villagers to spin and weave the cloth for their own clothes during their spare time from their agricultural pursuits.

Since these measures would answer the questions of employment, food and clothing, the village could then, through cooperative action, make just about everything that it would need or get it through barter or exchange from other villages. Accordingly, each village would be virtually self sufficient and would thus free itself from the domination of the urban centers that are today like evil loadstones drawing the people away from the rural areas, concentrating them in city slums and debauching them with urban vices. At least this is the argument of the Bhoodanists and other Gandhians.

Such ideas sound strange and archaic to Western ears. However, the

Indians have already achieved greater results than we Americans would ever expect. For example, millions of acres of land have been given up by rich landlords and additional millions of acres have been given up to cooperative management by small farmers. On the other hand, the Bhoodanists shrink from giving their movement the organization and drive that we in America would venture to guess that it must have in order to keep pace with the magnitude of the problems that everybody is trying to solve.

Even the government's five-year plans fall short in that they do not appear to be of sufficient scope to embrace their objectives. Thus, the three five-year plans were designed to provide 25,000,000 new jobs over a 15 year period but the birth rate of India is 6,000,000 per year. This means that in 15 years there will be 9[0],000,000 more people (less those who have died or retired) looking for the [25] million new jobs. In other words, if the planning were 100 per cent successful, it could not keep pace with the growth of problems it is trying to solve.

As for what should be done, we surely do not have the answer. But we do feel certain that India needs help. She must have outside capital and technical know-how. It is in the interest of the United States and the West to help supply these needs and *not attach strings to the gifts.*

Whatever we do should be done in a spirit of international brotherhood, not national selfishness. It should be done not merely because it is diplomatically expedient, but because it is morally compelling. At the same time, it will rebound to the credit of the West if India is able to maintain her democracy while solving her problems.

It would be a boon to democracy if one of the great nations of the world, with almost 400,000,000 people, proves that it is possible to provide a good living for everyone without surrendering to a dictatorship of either the "right" or "left." Today India is a tremendous force for peace and non-violence, at home and abroad. It is a land where the idealist and the intellectual are yet respected. We should want to help India preserve her soul and thus help to save our own.

Reflection Questions

1. Why did Dr. King value Gandhi's teachings?

2. What is a caste system and who are the "untouchables"? At the time Dr. King was writing, how were the experiences of the "untouchables" in India similar to the experiences of black people in the United States? How were they different?

3. What does Dr. King suggest Americans could learn from India? Do you find his suggestions reasonable?

4. If Dr. King and Gandhi were to have a conversation today, what might they talk about? What problems would they want to resolve?

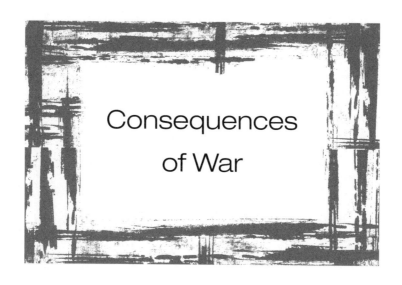

Consequences
of War

Beyond Vietnam:
A Time to Break Silence

Although Dr. King was critical of President Lyndon Johnson's escalation of American military involvement in Vietnam during the mid-1960s, he did not begin to speak publicly against the war until 1967. He delivered the following speech on April 4, 1967, to an audience of about three thousand at Riverside Church in New York City. Dr. King drafted it with the help of advisors including Spelman College professor Vincent Harding and Wesleyan University professor John Maguire, and insisted that he could not call upon discontented young blacks in American cities to use nonviolent tactics "without having first spoken clearly to the greatest purveyor of violence in the world: my own government." Many politicians and civil rights leaders criticized Dr. King's antiwar stand, but he was undeterred and continued to speak out against the war until his death.

I come to this magnificent house of worship tonight because my conscience leaves me no other choice. I join with you in this meeting because I am in deepest agreement with the aims and work of the organization which has brought us together: Clergy and [Laity] Concerned

---

Delivered at Riverside Church, New York City, April 4, 1967.
This version was published in "A Single Garment of Destiny":
A Global Vision of Justice *(Boston: Beacon Press, 2012).*

About Vietnam. The recent statement of your executive committee are the sentiments of my own heart and I found myself in full accord when I read its opening lines: "A time comes when silence is betrayal." That time has come for us in relation to Vietnam.

The truth of these words is beyond doubt, but the mission to which they call us is a most difficult one. Even when pressed by the demands of inner truth, men do not easily assume the task of opposing their government's policy, especially in [a] time of war. Nor does the human spirit move without great difficulty against all the apathy of conformist thought within one's own bosom and in the surrounding world. Moreover when the issues at hand seem as perplexing as they often do in the case of this dreadful conflict we are always on the verge of being mesmerized by uncertainty: but we must move on.

Some of us who have already begun to break the silence of the night have found that the calling to speak is often a vocation of agony, but we must speak. We must speak with all the humility that is appropriate to our limited vision, but we must speak. And we must rejoice as well, for surely this is the first time in our nation's history that a significant number of its religious leaders have chosen to move beyond the prophesying of smooth patriotism to the high grounds of a firm dissent based upon the mandates of conscience and the reading of history. Perhaps a new spirit is rising among us. If it is, let us trace its movement well and pray that our own inner being may be sensitive to its guidance, for we are deeply in need of a new way beyond the darkness that seems so close around us.

Over the past two years, as I have moved to break the betrayal of my own silences and to speak from the burnings of my own heart, as I have called for radical departures from the destruction of Vietnam, many persons have questioned me about the wisdom of my path. At the heart of their concerns this query has often loomed large and loud: Why are *you* speaking about the war, Dr. King? Why are *you* joining the voices of dissent? Peace and civil rights don't mix, they say. Aren't you hurting the cause of your people, they ask? And when I hear them, though I often understand the sources of their concern, I am nevertheless greatly saddened, for such questions mean that the inquirers have not really known me, my commitment or my calling. Indeed, their questions suggest that they do not know the world in which they live.

In the light of such tragic misunderstanding, I deem it of signal importance to try to state clearly, and I trust concisely, why I believe that the path from Dexter Avenue Baptist Church—the church in Montgomery, Alabama, where I began my pastorate—leads clearly to this sanctuary tonight.

I come to this platform tonight to make a passionate plea to my beloved nation. This speech is not addressed to Hanoi or to the National Liberation Front. It is not addressed to China or to Russia.

Nor is it an attempt to overlook the ambiguity of the total situation and the need for a collective solution to the tragedy of Vietnam. Neither is it an attempt to make North Vietnam or the National Liberation Front paragons of virtue, nor to overlook the role they can play in a successful resolution of the problem. While they both may have justifiable reason to be suspicious of the good faith of the United States, life and history give eloquent testimony to the fact that conflicts are never resolved without trustful give and take on both sides.

Tonight, however, I wish not to speak with Hanoi and the NLF, but rather to my fellow Americans who, with me, bear the greatest responsibility in ending a conflict that has exacted a heavy price on both continents.

Since I am a preacher by trade, I suppose it is not surprising that I have several reasons for bringing Vietnam into the field of my moral vision. There is at the outset a very obvious and almost facile connection between the war in Vietnam and the struggle I, and others, have been waging in America. A few years ago there was a shining moment in that struggle. It seemed as if there was a real promise of hope for the poor—both black and white—through the Poverty Program. There were experiments, hopes, new beginnings. Then came the build-up in Vietnam and I watched the program broken and eviscerated as if it were some idle political plaything of a society gone mad on war, and I knew that America would never invest the necessary funds or energies in rehabilitation of its poor so long as adventures like Vietnam continued to draw men and skills and money like some demoniacal destructive suction tube. So I was increasingly compelled to see the war as an enemy of the poor and to attack it as such.

Perhaps the more tragic recognition of reality took place when it became clear to me that the war was doing far more than devastating the hopes of the poor at home. It was sending their sons and their brothers and their husbands to fight and to die in extraordinarily high proportions relative to the rest of the population. We were taking the black young men who had been crippled by our society and sending them 8,000 miles away to guarantee liberties in Southeast Asia which they had not found in Southwest Georgia and East Harlem. So we have been repeatedly faced with the cruel irony of watching Negro and white boys on TV screens as they kill and die together for a nation that has been unable to seat them together in the same schools. So we watch them in brutal solidarity burning the huts of a poor village but we realize that they would never live on the same block in Detroit. I could not be silent in the face of such cruel manipulation of the poor.

My third reason moves to an even deeper level of awareness, for it grows out of my experience in the ghettos of the north over the last three years—especially the last three summers. As I have walked among the desperate, rejected and angry young men I have told them that Molotov cocktails and rifles would not solve their problems. I have tried to offer them my deepest compassion while maintaining my conviction that social change comes most meaningfully through non-violent action. But they asked—and rightly so—what about Vietnam? They asked if our own nation wasn't using massive doses of violence to solve its problems, to bring about the changes it wanted. Their questions hit home, and I knew that I could never again raise my voice against the violence of the oppressed in the ghettos without having first spoken clearly to the greatest purveyor of violence in the world today—my own government.

For the sake of those boys, for the sake of this government, for the sake of the hundreds of thousands trembling under our violence, I cannot be silent.

For those who ask the question, "Aren't you a Civil Rights leader?" and thereby mean to exclude me from the movement for peace, I have this further answer. In 1957 when a group of us formed the Southern Christian Leadership Conference, we chose as our motto: "To save the soul of America." We were convinced that we could not limit our vision to certain rights for black people, but instead affirmed the conviction that America would never be free or saved from itself until the descendants of its slaves were loosed completely from the shackles they still wear. In a way we were agreeing with Langston Hughes, that black bard of Harlem, who had written earlier:

> O, yes,
> I say it plain,
> America never was America to me,
> And yet I swear this oath—
> America will be!

Now, it should be incandescently clear that no one who has any concern for the integrity and life of America today can ignore the present war. If America's soul becomes totally poisoned, part of the autopsy must read Vietnam. It can never be saved so long as it destroys the deepest hopes of men the world over. So it is that those of us who are yet determined that America *will* be are led down the path of protest and dissent, working for the health of our land.

As if the weight of such a commitment to the life and health of America were not enough, another burden of responsibility was placed upon me in 1964; and I cannot forget that the Nobel Prize for Peace was also a commission—a commission to work harder than I had ever worked before for "the brotherhood of man." This is a calling that takes me beyond national allegiances, but even if it were not present I would yet have to live with the meaning of my commitment to the ministry of

Jesus Christ. To me the relationship of this ministry to the making of peace is so obvious that I sometimes marvel at those who ask me why I am speaking against the war. Could it be that they do not know that the good news was meant for all men—for communist and capitalist, for their children and ours, for black and for white, for revolutionary and conservative? Have they forgotten that my ministry is in obedience to the one who loved his enemies so fully that he died for them? What then can I say to the "Vietcong" or to Castro or to Mao as a faithful minister of this one? Can I threaten them with death or must I not share with them my life?

Finally, as I try to delineate for you and for myself the road that leads from Montgomery to this place I would have offered all that was most valid if I simply said that I must be true to my conviction that I share with all men the calling to be a son of the Living God. Beyond the calling of race or nation or creed is this vocation of sonship and brotherhood, and because I believe that the Father is deeply concerned especially for his suffering and helpless and outcast children, I come tonight to speak for them.

This I believe to be the privilege and the burden of all of us who deem ourselves bound by allegiances and loyalties which are broader and deeper than nationalism and which go beyond our nation's self-defined goals and positions. We are called to speak for the weak, for the voiceless, for the victims of our nation and for those it calls enemy, for no document from human hands can make these humans any less our brothers.

And as I ponder the madness of Vietnam and search within myself for ways to understand and respond in compassion my mind goes constantly to the people of that peninsula. I speak now not of the soldiers of each side, not of the junta in Saigon, but simply of the people who have been living under the curse of war for almost three continuous decades now. I think of them too because it is clear to me that there will be no meaningful solution there until some attempt is made to know them and hear their broken cries.

They must see Americans as strange liberators. The Vietnamese people proclaimed their own independence in 1945 after a combined French and Japanese occupation, and before the communist revolution in China. They were led by Ho Chi Minh. Even though they quoted the American Declaration of Independence in their own document of freedom, we refused to recognize them. Instead, we decided to support France in its re-conquest of her former colony.

Our government felt then that the Vietnamese people were not "ready" for independence, and we again fell victim to the deadly western arrogance that has poisoned the international atmosphere for so long. With that tragic decision we rejected a revolutionary government seeking self-determination, and a government that had been established not by China (for whom the Vietnamese have no great love) but by clearly indigenous forces that included some communists. For the peasants this new government meant real land reform, one of the most important needs in their lives.

For nine years following 1945 we denied the people of Vietnam the right of independence. For nine years we vigorously supported the French in their abortive effort to re-colonize Vietnam.

Before the end of the war we were meeting 80% of the French war costs. Even before the French were defeated at Dien Bien Phu, they began to despair of the reckless action, but we did not. We encouraged them with our huge financial and military supplies to continue the war even after they had lost the will. Soon we would be paying almost the full costs of this tragic attempt at re-colonization.

After the French were defeated it looked as if independence and land reform would come again through the Geneva agreements. But instead there came the United States, determined that Ho should not unify the temporarily divided nation, and the peasants watched again as we supported one of the most vicious modern dictators—our chosen man, Premier Diem. The peasants watched and cringed as Diem ruthlessly routed out all opposition, supported their extortionist landlords and refused even to discuss re-unification with the North. The peasants watched as all this was presided over by U.S. influence and then by increasing numbers of U.S. troops who came to help quell the insurgency that Diem's methods had aroused. When Diem was overthrown they may have been happy, but the long line of military dictatorships seemed to offer no real change—especially in terms of their need for land and peace.

The only change came from America as we increased our troop commitments in support of governments which were singularly corrupt, inept and without popular support. All the while the people read our leaflets and received regular promises of peace and democracy—and land reform. Now they languish under our bombs and consider us—not their fellow Vietnamese—the real enemy. They move sadly and apathetically as we herd them off the land of their fathers into concentration camps where minimal social needs are rarely met. They know they must move or be destroyed by our bombs. So they go—primarily women and children and the aged.

They watch as we poison their water, as we kill a million acres of their crops. They must weep as the bulldozers roar through their areas preparing to destroy the precious trees. They wander into the hospitals, with at least 20 casualties from American firepower for one "Vietcong"-inflicted injury. They wander into the towns and see thousands of the children, homeless, without clothes, running in packs on the streets like animals. They see the children degraded by our soldiers as they beg for food. They see the children selling their sisters to our soldiers, soliciting for their mothers.

What do the peasants think as we ally ourselves with the landlords and as we refuse to put any action into our many words concerning land reform? What do they think as we test out our latest weapons on them, just as the Germans tested out new medicine and new tortures in the concentration camps of Europe? Where are the roots of the independent Vietnam we claim to be building? Is it among these voiceless ones?

We have destroyed their two most cherished institutions: the family and the village. We have destroyed their land and their crops. We have cooperated in the crushing of the nation's only non-Communist revolutionary political force—the unified Buddhist Church. We have supported the enemies of the peasants of Saigon. We have corrupted their women and children and killed their men. What liberators!

Now there is little left to build on—save bitterness. Soon the only solid physical foundations remaining will be found at our military bases and in the concrete of the concentration camps we call fortified hamlets. The peasants may well wonder if we plan to build our new Vietnam on such grounds as these? Could we blame them for such thoughts? We must speak for them and raise the questions they cannot raise. These too are our brothers.

Perhaps the more difficult but no less necessary task is to speak for those who have been designated as our enemies. What of the National Liberation Front—that strangely anonymous group we call VC or Communists? What must they think of us in America when they realize that we permitted the repression and cruelty of Diem which helped to bring them into being as a resistance group in the south? What do they think of our condoning the violence which led to their own taking up of arms? How can they believe in our integrity when now we speak of "aggression from the North" as if there were nothing more essential to the war? How can they trust us when now we charge them with violence after the murderous reign of Diem, and charge them with violence while we pour every new weapon of death into their land? Surely we must understand their feelings even if we do not condone their actions. Surely we must see that the men we supported pressed them to their violence. Surely we must see that our own computerized plans of destruction simply dwarf their greatest acts.

How do they judge us when our officials know that their membership is less than 25 per cent communist and yet insist on giving them the blanket name? What must they be thinking when they know that we are aware of their control of major sections of Vietnam and yet we appear ready to allow national elections in which this highly organized political parallel government will have no part? They ask how we can speak of free elections when the Saigon press is censored and controlled by the military junta. And they are surely right to wonder what kind of new government we plan to help form without them—the only party in real touch with the peasants. They question our political goals and they deny the reality of a peace settlement from which they will be excluded. Their questions are frighteningly relevant. Is our nation planning to build on political myth again and then shore it up with the power of new violence?

Here is the true meaning and value of compassion and nonviolence when it helps us to see the enemy's point of view, to hear his questions, to know his assessment of ourselves. For from his view we may indeed see the basic weaknesses of our own condition, and if we are mature, we may learn and grow and profit from the wisdom of the brothers who are called the opposition.

So, too, with Hanoi. In the North, where our bombs now pummel the land, and our mines endanger the waterways, we are met by a deep but understandable mistrust. To speak for them is to explain this lack of confidence in western words, and especially their distrust of American intentions now. In Hanoi are the men who led the nation to independence against the Japanese and the French, the men who sought membership in the French commonwealth and were betrayed by the weakness of Paris and the willfulness of the colonial armies. It was they who led a second struggle against French domination at tremendous costs, and then were persuaded to give up the land they controlled between the 13th and 17th parallel as a temporary measure at Geneva. After 1954 they watched us conspire with Diem to prevent elections which would have surely brought Ho Chi Minh to power over a united Vietnam, and they realized they had been betrayed again.

When we ask why they do not leap to negotiate, these things must be remembered. Also it must be clear that the leaders of Hanoi considered the presence of American troops in support of the Diem regime to have been the initial military breach of the Geneva Agreements concerning foreign troops, and they remind us that they did not begin to send in any large number of supplies or men until American forces had moved into the tens of thousands.

Hanoi remembers how our leaders refused to tell us the truth about the earlier North Vietnamese overtures for peace, how we claimed that none existed when they had clearly been made. Ho Chi Minh has watched as America has spoken of peace and built up its forces, and now he has surely heard of the increasing international rumors of American plans for an invasion of the North. Perhaps only his sense of humor and irony can save him when he hears the most powerful nation of the world speaking of *his* aggression as it drops thousands of bombs on a poor weak nation more than 8,000 miles away from its shores.

At this point I should make it clear that while I have tried in these last few minutes to give a voice to the voiceless on Vietnam and to understand the arguments of those who are called enemy, I am as deeply concerned about our own troops there as anything else. For it occurs to me that what we are submitting them to in Vietnam is not simply the brutalizing process that goes on in any war where armies face each other and seek to destroy. We are adding cynicism to the process of death, for they must know after a short period there that none of the things we claim to be fighting for are really involved. Before long they must know that their government has sent them into a struggle among Vietnamese, and the more sophisticated surely realize that we are on the side of the wealthy and the secure while we create a hell for the poor.

Somehow this madness must cease. We must stop now. I speak as a child of God and brother to the suffering poor of Vietnam. I speak for those whose land is being laid waste, whose homes are being destroyed, whose culture is being subverted. I speak for the poor of America who are paying the double price of smashed hopes at home and death and corruption in Vietnam. I speak as a citizen of the world, for the world as it stands aghast at the path we have taken. I speak as an American to the leaders of my own nation. The great initiative in this war is ours. The initiative to stop it must be ours.

This is the message of the great Buddhist leaders of Vietnam. Recently one of them wrote these words: "Each day the war goes on the hatred increases in the heart of the Vietnamese and in the hearts of those of humanitarian instinct. The Americans are forcing even their friends into becoming their enemies. It is curious that the Americans, who calculate so carefully on the possibilities of military victory, do not realize that in the process they are incurring deep psychological and political defeat. The image of America will never again be the image of revolution, freedom and democracy, but the image of violence and militarism."

If we continue there will be no doubt in my mind and in the mind of the world that we have no honorable intentions in Vietnam. It will become clear that our minimal expectation is to occupy it as an American colony and men will not refrain from thinking that our maximum hope is to goad China into a war so that we may bomb her nuclear installations. If we do not stop our war against the people of Vietnam immediately the world will be left with no other alternative than to see this as some horribly clumsy and deadly game we have decided to play.

The world now demands a maturity of America that we may not be able to achieve. It demands that we admit that we have been wrong from the beginning of our adventure in Vietnam, that we have been detrimental to the life of the Vietnamese people.

In order to atone for our sins and errors in Vietnam, we should take the initiative in bringing a halt to this tragic war. I would like to suggest five concrete things that our government should do immediately to begin the long and difficult process of extricating ourselves from this nightmarish conflict:

1. End all bombing in North and South Vietnam.

2. Declare a unilateral cease-fire in the hope that such action will create the atmosphere for negotiation.

3. Take immediate steps to prevent other battlegrounds in Southeast Asia by curtailing our military build-up in Thailand and our interference in Laos.

4. Realistically accept the fact that the National Liberation Front has substantial support in South Vietnam and must thereby play a role in any meaningful negotiations and in any future Vietnam government.

5. Set a date that we will remove all foreign troops from Vietnam in accordance with the 1954 Geneva Agreement.

Part of our ongoing commitment might well express itself in an offer to grant asylum to any Vietnamese who fears for his life under a new regime which included the Liberation Front. Then we must make what reparations we can for the damage we have done. We must provide the medical aid that is badly needed, making it available in this country if necessary.

Meanwhile we in the churches and synagogues have a continuing task while we urge our government to disengage itself from a disgraceful commitment. We must continue to raise our voices if our nation persists in its perverse ways in Vietnam. We must be prepared to match actions with words by seeking out every creative means of protest possible.

As we counsel young men concerning military service we must clarify for them our nation's role in Vietnam and challenge them with the alternative of conscientious objection. I am pleased to say that this is the path now being chosen by more than seventy students at my own Alma Mater, Morehouse College, and I recommend it to all who find the American course in Vietnam a dishonorable and unjust one. Moreover I would encourage all ministers of draft age to give up their ministerial exemptions and seek status as conscientious objectors. These are the times for real choices and not false ones. We are at the moment when our lives must be placed on the line if our nation is to survive its own folly. Every man of humane convictions must decide on the protest that best suits his convictions, but we must all protest.

There is something seductively tempting about stopping there and sending us all off on what in some circles has become a popular crusade against the war in Vietnam. I say we must enter that struggle, but I wish to go on now to say something even more disturbing. The war in Vietnam is but a symptom of a far deeper malady within the American spirit, and if we ignore this sobering reality we will find ourselves organizing clergy- and laymen-concerned committees for the next generation. They will be concerned about Guatemala and Peru. They will be concerned about Thailand and Cambodia. They will be concerned about Mozambique and South Africa. We will be marching for these and a dozen other names and attending rallies without end unless there is a significant and profound change in American life and policy. Such thoughts take us beyond Vietnam, but not beyond our calling as sons of the living God.

In 1957 a sensitive American official overseas said that it seemed to him that our nation was on the wrong side of a world revolution. During the past 10 years we have seen emerge a pattern of suppression which now has justified the presence of U.S. military "advisors" in Venezuela. This need to maintain social stability for our investments accounts for the counter-revolutionary action of American forces in Guatemala. It tells why American helicopters are being used against guerrillas in Colombia and why American napalm and green beret forces have already been active against rebels in Peru. It is with such activity in mind that the words of the late John F. Kennedy come back to haunt us. Five years ago he said, "Those who make peaceful revolution impossible will make violent revolution inevitable."

Increasingly, by choice or by accident, this is the role our nation has taken—the role of those who make peaceful revolution impossible by refusing to give up the privileges and the pleasures that come from the immense profits of overseas investments.

I am convinced that if we are to get on the right side of the world revolution, we as a nation must undergo a radical revolution of values. We must rapidly begin the shift from a "thing-oriented" society to a "person-oriented" society. When machines and computers, profit motives and property rights are considered more important than people, the giant triplets of racism, materialism, and militarism are incapable of being conquered.

A true revolution of values will soon cause us to question the fairness and justice of many of our past and present policies. On the one hand we are called to play the Good Samaritan on life's roadside; but that will be only an initial act. One day we must come to see that the whole Jericho Road must be transformed so that men and women will not be constantly beaten and robbed as they make their journey on Life's highway. True compassion is more than flinging a coin to a beggar; it is not haphazard and superficial. It comes to see that an edifice which produces beggars needs re-structuring. A true revolution of values will soon look uneasily on the glaring contrast of poverty and wealth. With righteous indignation, it will look across the seas and see individual capitalists of the West investing huge sums of money in Asia, Africa and South America, only to take the profits out with no concern for the social betterment of the countries, and say: "This is not just." It will look at our alliance with the landed gentry of Latin America and say: "This is not just." The Western arrogance of feeling that it has everything to teach others and nothing to learn from them is not just. A true revolution of values will lay hands on the world order and say of war: "This way of settling differences is not just." This business of burning human beings with napalm, of filling our nation's homes with orphans and widows, of injecting poisonous drugs of hate into veins of peoples normally humane, of sending men home from dark and bloody battlefields physically handicapped and psychologically deranged, cannot be reconciled with wisdom, justice, and love. A nation that continues year after year to spend more money on military defense than on programs of social uplift is approaching spiritual death.

America, the richest and most powerful nation in the world, can well lead the way in this revolution of values. There is nothing, except a tragic death wish, to prevent us from reordering our priorities, so that the pursuit of peace will take precedence over the pursuit of war. There is nothing to keep us from molding a recalcitrant status-quo with bruised hands until we have fashioned it into a brotherhood.

This kind of positive revolution of values is our best defense against Communism. War is not the answer. Communism will never be defeated by the use of atomic bombs or nuclear weapons. Let us not join those who shout war and through their misguided passions urge the United States to relinquish its participation in the United Nations. These are days which demand wise restraint and calm reasonableness. We must not call everyone a Communist or an appeaser who advocates the seating of Red China in the United Nations and who recognizes that hate and hysteria are not the final answers to the problem of these turbulent days. We must not engage in a negative anti-Communism, but rather in a positive thrust for democracy, realizing that our greatest defense against Communism is to take offensive action in behalf of justice. We must with positive action seek to remove those conditions of poverty, insecurity and injustice which are the fertile soil in which the seed of Communism grows and develops.

These are revolutionary times. All over the globe men are revolting against old systems of exploitation and oppression and out of the wombs of a frail world new systems of justice and equality are being born. The shirtless and barefoot people of the land are rising up as never before. "The people who sat in darkness have seen a great light." We in the West must support these revolutions. It is a sad fact that, because of comfort, complacency, a morbid fear of Communism, and our proneness to adjust to injustice, the Western nations that initiated so much of the revolutionary spirit of the modern world have now become the arch anti-revolutionaries. This has driven many to feel that only Marxism has the revolutionary spirit. Therefore, Communism is a judgment against our failure to make democracy real and follow through on the revolutions that we initiated. Our only hope today lies in our ability to recapture the revolutionary spirit and go out into a sometimes hostile world declaring eternal hostility to poverty, racism, and militarism. With this powerful commitment we shall boldly challenge the status-quo and unjust mores and thereby speed the day when "every valley shall be exalted, and every mountain and hill shall be made low, and the crooked shall be made straight and the rough places plain."

A genuine revolution of values means in the final analysis that our loyalties must become ecumenical rather than sectional. Every nation must now develop an overriding loyalty to mankind as a whole in order to preserve the best in their individual societies.

This call for a world-wide fellowship that lifts neighborly concern beyond one's tribe, race, class and nation is in reality a call for an all-embracing and unconditional love for all men. This oft misunderstood and misinterpreted concept—so readily dismissed by the Nietzsches of the world as a weak and cowardly force—has now become an absolute necessity for the survival of man. When I speak of love I am not speaking of some sentimental and weak response. I am speaking of that force which all of the great religions have seen as the supreme unifying principle of life. Love is somehow the key that unlocks the door which leads to ultimate reality. This Hindu-Moslem-Christian-Jewish-Buddhist belief about ultimate reality is beautifully summed up in the first epistle of Saint John:

> Let us love one another; for love is God and everyone that loveth is born of God and knoweth God. He that loveth not knoweth not God; for God is love. If we love one another, God dwelleth in us, and his love is perfected in us.

Let us hope that this spirit will become the order of the day. We can no longer afford to worship the God of hate or bow before the altar of retaliation. The oceans of history are made turbulent by the ever-rising tides of hate. History is cluttered with the wreckage of nations and individuals that pursued this self-defeating path of hate. As Arnold Toynbee says: "Love is the ultimate force that makes for the saving choice of life and good against the damning choice of death and evil. Therefore the first hope in our inventory must be the hope that love is going to have the last word."

We are now faced with the fact that tomorrow is today. We are confronted with the fierce urgency of now. In this unfolding conundrum of life and history there is such a thing as being too late. Procrastination is still the thief of time. Life often leaves us standing bare, naked and dejected with a lost opportunity. The "tide in the affairs of men" does not remain at the flood; it ebbs. We may cry out desperately for time to pause in her passage, but time is deaf to every plea and rushes on. Over the bleached bones and jumbled residue of numerous civilizations are written the pathetic words: "Too late." There is an invisible book of life that faithfully records our vigilance or our neglect. "The moving finger writes, and having writ moves on." We still have a choice today: non-violent co-existence or violent co-annihilation.

We must move past indecision to action. We must find new ways to speak for peace in Vietnam and justice throughout the developing world—a world that borders on our doors. If we do not act we shall surely be dragged down the long dark and shameful corridors of time reserved for those who possess power without compassion, might without morality, and strength without sight.

Now let us begin. Now let us re-dedicate ourselves to the long and bitter—but beautiful—struggle for a new world. This is the calling of the sons of God, and our brothers wait eagerly for our response. Shall we say the odds are too great? Shall we tell them the struggle is too hard? Will our message be that the forces of American life militate against their arrival as full men, and we send our deepest regrets? Or will there be another message, of longing, of hope, of solidarity with their yearnings, of commitment to their cause, whatever the cost? The choice is ours, and though we might prefer it otherwise we *must* choose in this crucial moment of human history.

Reflection Questions

1. Why did Dr. King speak out against the Vietnam War? How was his stance against the war related to his stand against racial oppression in the United States?

2. Dr. King writes that "compassion and nonviolence [help] us to see the enemy's point of view, to hear his questions, to know his assessment of ourselves." Why do you think Dr. King puts so much importance on looking at things from the perspective of the "enemy"? What is accomplished by doing so?

3. What kind of revolution does Dr. King call for? Do you think such a revolution is possible? What is one change that you would make in today's world to help bring about the revolution Dr. King describes?

4. Do you think the United States learned the lessons Dr. King taught in this piece? Explain your reasoning.

The Casualties of the
War in Vietnam

On February 25, 1967, Dr. King addressed the Nation Institute in Los Angeles where he questioned the United States' military intervention against Communist-led nationalists fighting the American-supported government in South Vietnam. Although Dr. King supported Lyndon Johnson's "war against poverty," he risked his relationship with the president by opposing his war policies, which Dr. King saw as taking resources from domestic programs.

I need not pause to say how happy I am to have the privilege of being a participant in this significant symposium. In these days of emotional tension when the problems of the world are gigantic in extent and chaotic in detail, there is no greater need than for sober-thinking, healthy debate, creative dissent and enlightened discussion. This is why this symposium is so important.

I would like to speak to you candidly and forthrightly this afternoon about our present involvement in Vietnam. I have chosen as a subject, "The Casualties of the War in Vietnam." We are all aware of the nightmarish physical casualties. We see them in our living rooms in all of their tragic dimensions on television screens, and we read about them

Delivered at the Nation Institute, Beverly-Hilton Hotel,
Los Angeles, California, February 25, 1967.

on our subway and bus rides in daily newspaper accounts. We see the rice fields of a small Asian country being trampled at will and burned at whim: we see grief-stricken mothers with crying babies clutched in their arms as they watch their little huts burst forth into flames; we see the fields and valleys of battle being painted with humankind's blood; we see the broken bodies left prostrate in countless fields; we see young men being sent home half-men—physically handicapped and mentally deranged. Most tragic of all is the casualty list among children. Some one million Vietnamese children have been casualties of this brutal war. A war in which children are incinerated by napalm, in which American soldiers die in mounting numbers while other American soldiers, according to press accounts, in unrestrained hatred shoot the wounded enemy as they lie on the ground, is a war that mutilates the conscience. These casualties are enough to cause all men to rise up with righteous indignation and oppose the very nature of this war.

But the physical casualties of the war in Vietnam are not alone the catastrophes. The casualties of principles and values are equally disastrous and injurious. Indeed, they are ultimately more harmful because they are self-perpetuating. If the casualties of principle are not healed, the physical casualties will continue to mount.

One of the first casualties of the war in Vietnam was the Charter of the United Nations. In taking armed action against the Vietcong and North Vietnam, the United States clearly violated the United Nations charter which provides, in chapter I, article II, "All members shall refrain in their international relations from the threat or use of force against the territorial integrity or political independence of any state or in any other manner inconsistent with the purposes of the United Nations"; and in chapter VII, "The Security Council shall determine the existence of any threat to the peace, breach of the peace, or act of aggression, and shall make recommendations or shall decide what measures shall be taken ... to maintain or restore international peace and security."

It is very obvious that our government blatantly violated its obligation under the charter of the United Nations to submit to the Security

Council its charge of aggression against North Vietnam. Instead we unilaterally launched an all-out war on Asian soil. In the process we have undermined the purpose of the United Nations and caused its effectiveness to atrophy. We have also placed our nation in the position of being morally and politically isolated. Even the long-standing allies of our nation have adamantly refused to join our government in this ugly war. As Americans and lovers of Democracy we should carefully ponder the consequences of our nation's declining moral status in the world.

The second casualty of the war in Vietnam is the principle of self-determination. By entering a war that is little more than a domestic civil war, America has ended up supporting a new form of colonialism covered up by certain niceties of complexity. Whether we realize it or not our participation in the war in Vietnam is an ominous expression of our lack of sympathy for the oppressed, our paranoid anti-Communism, our failure to feel the ache and anguish of the have-nots. It reveals our willingness to continue participating in neo-colonialist adventures.

A brief look at the background and history of this war reveals with brutal clarity [the] ugliness of our policy. The Vietnamese people proclaimed their own independence in 1945 after a combined French and Japanese occupation, and before the Communist revolution in China. They were led by the now well-known Ho Chi Minh. Even though they quoted the American Declaration of Independence in their own document of freedom, we refused to recognize them. Instead, we decided to support France in its re-conquest of her former colony.

President Truman felt then that the Vietnamese people were not "ready" for independence, and we again fell victim to the deadly Western arrogance that has poisoned the international atmosphere for so long. With that tragic decision we rejected a revolutionary government seeking self-determination, and a government that had been established not by China (for whom the Vietnamese have no great love) but by clearly indigenous forces that included some Communists.

For nine years following 1945 we denied the people of Vietnam the right to independence. For nine years we vigorously supported the French in their abortive effort to re-colonize Vietnam.

Before the end of the war we were meeting 80% of the French war costs. Even before the French were defeated at Dien Bien Phu, they began to despair of their reckless action, but we did not. We encouraged them with our huge financial and military supplies to continue the war even after they had lost the will.

During this period United States governmental officials began to brainwash the American public. John Foster Dulles assiduously sought to prove that Indo-China was essential to our security against the Chinese Communist peril. When a negotiated settlement of the war was reached in 1954, through the Geneva Accord, it was done against our will. After doing all that we could to sabotage the planning for the Geneva Accord, we finally refused to sign it.

Soon after this we helped install Ngo Dinh Diem. We supported him in his betrayal of the Geneva Accord and his refusal to have the promised 1956 elections. We watched with approval as he engaged in ruthless and bloody persecution of all opposition forces. When Diem's infamous actions finally led to the formation of the National Liberation Front, the American public was duped into believing that the civil rebellion was being waged by puppets from Hanoi. As Douglas Pike wrote: "In horror, Americans helplessly watched Diem tear apart the fabric of Vietnamese society more effectively than the Communists had ever been able to do it. It was the most efficient act of his entire career."

Since Diem's death we have actively supported another dozen military dictatorships all in the name of fighting for freedom. When it became evident that these regimes could not defeat the Vietcong, we began to steadily increase our forces, calling them "military advisors" rather than fighting soldiers.

Today we are fighting an all-out war—undeclared by Congress. We have well over 300,000 American servicemen fighting in that benighted and unhappy country. American planes are bombing the territory of another country, and we are committing atrocities equal to any perpe-trated by the Vietcong. This is the third largest war in American history.

All of this reveals that we are in an untenable position morally and politically. We are left standing before the world glutted by our barbar-ity. We are engaged in a war that seeks to turn the clock of history back and perpetuate white colonialism. The greatest irony and tragedy of all is that our nation which initiated so much of the revolutionary spirit of the modern world, is [now] cast in the mold of being an arch anti-revolutionary.

A third casualty of the war in Vietnam is the Great Society. This con-fused war has played havoc with our domestic destinies.

Despite feeble protestations to the contrary, the promises of the Great Society have been shot down on the battlefield of Vietnam. The pursuit of this widened war has narrowed domestic welfare programs, making the poor, white and Negro, bear the heaviest burdens both at the front and at home.

While the anti-poverty program is cautiously initiated, zealously su-pervised and evaluated for immediate results, billions are liberally ex-pended for this ill-considered war. The recently revealed mis-estimate of the war budget amounts to ten billions [sic] of dollars for a single year. This error alone is more than five times the amount committed to anti-poverty programs. The security we profess to seek in foreign adventures we will lose in our decaying cities. The bombs in Vietnam explode at home: they destroy the hopes and possibilities for a decent America.

If we reversed investments and gave the armed forces the anti-poverty budget, the generals could be forgiven if they walked off the battlefield in disgust.

Poverty, urban problems and social progress generally are ignored when the guns of war become a national obsession. When it is not our security that is at stake, but questionable and vague commitments to reactionary regimes, values disintegrate into foolish and adolescent slogans.

It is estimated that we spend $322,000 for each enemy we kill, while we spend in the so-called war on poverty in America only about $53.00 for each person classified as "poor." And much of that 53 dollars goes for salaries of people who are not poor. We have escalated the war in Vietnam and de-escalated the skirmish against poverty. It challenges the imagination to contemplate what lives we could transform if we were to cease killing.

At this moment in history it is irrefutable that our world prestige is pathetically frail. Our war policy excites pronounced contempt and aversion virtually everywhere. Even when some national governments, for reasons of economic and diplomatic interest, do not condemn us, their people in surprising measure have made clear they do not share the official policy.

We are isolated in our false values in a world demanding social and economic justice. We must undergo a vigorous re-ordering of our national priorities.

A fourth casualty of the war in Vietnam is the humility of our nation. Through rugged determination, scientific and technological progress and dazzling achievements, America has become the richest and most powerful nation in the world. We have built machines that think and instruments that peer into the unfathomable ranges of interstellar space. We have built gargantuan bridges to span the seas and gigantic buildings to kiss the skies. Through our airplanes and spaceships we have dwarfed distance and placed time in chains, and through our submarines we have penetrated oceanic depths. This year our national gross product will reach the astounding figure of 780 billion dollars. All of this is a staggering picture of our great power.

But honesty impels me to admit that our power has often made us arrogant. We feel that our money can do anything. We arrogantly feel that we have everything to teach other nations and nothing to learn from them. We often arrogantly feel that we have some divine, messianic mission to police the whole world. We are arrogant in not allowing young nations to go through the same growing pains, turbulence and revolution that characterized our history. We are arrogant in our contention that we have some sacred mission to protect people from totalitarian rule, while we make little use of our power to end the evils of South Africa and Rhodesia, and while we are in fact supporting dictatorships with guns and money under the guise of fighting Communism. We are arrogant in professing to be concerned about the freedom of foreign nations while not setting our own house in order. Many of our Senators and Congressmen vote joyously to appropriate billions of dollars for war in Vietnam, and these same Senators and Congressmen vote loudly against a Fair Housing Bill to make it possible for a Negro veteran of Vietnam to purchase a decent home. We arm Negro soldiers to kill on foreign battlefields, but offer little protection for their relatives from beatings and killings in our own south. We are willing to make the Negro 100% of a citizen in warfare, but reduce him to 50% of a citizen on American soil. Of all the good things in life the Negro has approximately one half those of whites; of the bad he has twice that of whites. Thus, half of all Negroes live in substandard housing and Negroes have half the income of whites. When we turn to the negative experiences of life, the Negro has a double share. There are twice as many unemployed. The infant mortality rate is double that of white[s]. There are twice as many Negroes in combat in Vietnam at the beginning of 1967 and twice as many died in action (20.6%) in proportion to their numbers in the population as whites.

All of this reveals that our nation has not yet used its vast resources of power to end the long night of poverty, racism and man's inhumanity to man. Enlarged power means enlarged peril if there is not concomitant growth of the soul. Genuine power is the right use of strength. If our nation's strength is not used responsibly and with restraint, it will be, following Acton's dictum, power that tends to corrupt and absolute power that corrupts absolutely. Our arrogance can be our doom. It can bring the curtains down on our national drama. Ultimately a great nation is a compassionate nation. We are challenged in these turbulent days to use our power to speed up the day when "every valley shall be exalted, and every mountain and hill shall be made low: and the crooked shall be made straight, and the rough places plain."

A fifth casualty of the war in Vietnam is the principle of dissent. An ugly repressive sentiment to silence peace-seekers depicts advocates of immediate negotiation under terms of the Geneva agreement and persons who call for a cessation of bombings in the north as quasi-traitors, fools or venal enemies of our soldiers and institutions. Free speech and the privilege of dissent and discussion are rights being shot down by bombers in Vietnam. When those who stand for peace are so vilified it is time to consider where we are going and whether free speech has not become one of the major casualties of the war.

Curtailment of free speech is rationalized on grounds that a more compelling American tradition forbids criticism of the government when the nation is at war. More than a century ago when we were in a declared state of war with Mexico, a first term congressman by the name of Abraham Lincoln stood in the halls of Congress and fearlessly denounced that war. Congressman Abraham Lincoln of Illinois had not heard of this tradition or he was not inclined to respect it. Nor had Thoreau and Emerson and many other philosophers who shaped our democratic principles. Nothing can be more destructive of our fundamental democratic traditions than the vicious effort to silence dissenters.

A sixth casualty of the war in Vietnam is the prospect of mankind's survival. This war has created the climate for greater armament and further expansion of destructive nuclear power.

One of the most persistent ambiguities that we face is that everybody talks about peace as a goal. However, it does not take sharpest-eyed sophistication to discern that while everybody talks about peace, peace has become practically nobody's business among the power-wielders. Many men cry peace! peace! but they refuse to do the things that make for peace.

The large power blocs of the world talk passionately of pursuing peace while burgeoning defense budgets that already bulge, enlarging already awesome armies, and devising even more devastating weapons. Call the roll of those who sing the glad tidings of peace and one's ears will be surprised by the responding sounds. The heads of all of the nations issue clarion calls for peace yet these destiny determiners come accompanied by a band and a brigand of national choristers, each bearing unsheathed swords rather than olive branches.

The stages of history are replete with the chants and choruses of the conquerors of old who came killing in pursuit of peace. Alexander, Genghis Khan, Julius Caesar, Charlemagne, and Napoleon were akin in their seeking a peaceful world order, a world fashioned after their selfish conceptions of an ideal existence. Each sought a world at peace which would personify his egotistic dreams. Even within the life span of most of us, another megalomaniac strode across the world stage. He sent his blitzkrieg-bent legions blazing across Europe, bringing havoc and holocaust in his wake. There is grave irony in the fact that Hitler could come forth, following the nakedly aggressive expansionist theories he revealed in *Mein Kampf,* and do it all in the name of peace.

So when I see in this day the leaders of nations similarly talking peace while preparing for war, I take frightful pause. When I see our country today intervening in what is basically a civil war, destroying hundreds of thousands of Vietnamese children with napalm, leaving broken bodies in countless fields and sending home half-men, mutilated, mentally and physically; when I see the recalcitrant unwillingness of our govern-ment to create the atmosphere for a negotiated settlement of this awful conflict by halting bombings in the north and agreeing to talk with the Vietcong—and all this in the name of pursuing the goal of peace—I tremble for our world. I do so not only from dire recall of the nightmares wreaked in the wars of yesterday, but also from dreadful realization of today's possible nuclear destructiveness, and tomorrow's even more damnable prospects.

In the light of all this, I say that we must narrow the gaping chasm be-tween our proclamations of peace and our lowly deeds which precipitate and perpetuate war. We are called upon to look up from the quagmire of military programs and defense commitments and read history's signposts and today's trends.

The past is prophetic in that it asserts loudly that wars are poor chisels for carving out peaceful tomorrows. One day we must come to see that peace is not merely a distant goal that we seek, but a means by which we arrive at that goal. We must pursue peaceful ends through peaceful means. How much longer must we play at deadly war games before we heed the plaintive pleas of the unnumbered dead and maimed of past wars? Why can't we at long last grow up, and take off our blindfolds, chart new courses, put our hands to the rudder and set sail for the distant destination, the port city of peace?

President John F. Kennedy said on one occasion, "Mankind must put an end to war or war will put an end to mankind." Wisdom born of experience should tell us that war is obsolete. There may have been a time when war served as a negative good by preventing the spread and growth of an evil force, but the destructive power of modern weapons eliminates even the possibility that war may serve as a negative good. If we assume that life is worth living and that man has a right to survive, then we must find an alternative to war. In a day when vehicles hurtle through outer space and guided ballistic missiles carve highways of death through the stratosphere, no nation can claim victory in war. A so-called limited war will leave little more than a calamitous legacy of human suffering, political turmoil, and spiritual disillusionment. A world war—God forbid!—will leave only smoldering ashes as a mute testimony of a human race whose folly led inexorably to ultimate death. So if modern man continues to flirt unhesitatingly with war, he will transform his earthly habitat into an inferno such as even the mind of Dante could not imagine.

I do not wish to minimize the complexity of the problems that need to be faced in achieving disarmament and peace. But I think it is a fact that we shall not have the will, the courage and the insight to deal with such matters unless in this field we are prepared to undergo a mental and spiritual re-evaluation, a change of focus which will enable us to see that the things which seem most real and powerful are indeed now unreal and have come under the sentence of death. We need to make a supreme effort to generate the readiness, indeed the eagerness, to enter into the new world which is now possible.

We will not build a peaceful world by following a negative path. It is not enough to say "we must not wage war." It is necessary to love peace and sacrifice for it. We must concentrate not merely on the negative expulsion of war, but on the positive affirmation of peace. There is a fascinating little story that is preserved for us in Greek literature about Ulysses and the Sirens. The Sirens had the ability to sing so sweetly that sailors could not resist steering toward their island. Many ships were lured upon the rocks and the men forgot home, duty and honor as they flung themselves into the sea to be embraced by arms that drew them down to death. Ulysses, determined not to be lured by the Sirens, first decided to tie himself tightly to the mast of his boat and his crew stuffed their ears with wax. But finally he and his crew learned a better way to save themselves: they took on board the beautiful singer Orpheus whose melodies were sweeter than the music of the Sirens. When Orpheus sang, who bothered to listen to the Sirens? So we must fix our visions not merely on the negative expulsion of war but upon the positive affirmation of peace. We must see that peace represents a sweeter music, a cosmic melody that is far superior to the discords of war. Somehow we must transform the dynamics of the world power struggle from the negative nuclear arms race which no one can win to a positive contest to harness man's creative genius for the purpose of making peace and prosperity a reality for all of the nations of the world. In short, we must shift the arms race into a "peace race." If we have the will and determination to mount such a peace offensive we will unlock hitherto tightly sealed doors of hope and bring new light into the dark chambers of pessimism.

Let me say finally that I oppose the war in Vietnam because I love

America. I speak out against it not in anger but with anxiety and sorrow in my heart, and above all with a passionate desire to see our beloved country stand as the moral example of the world. I speak out against this war because I am disappointed with America. There can be no great disappointment where there is no great love. I am disappointed with our failure to deal positively and forthrightly with the triple evils of racism, extreme materialism and militarism. We are presently moving down a dead-end road that can lead to national disaster.

Jesus once told a parable of a young man who left home and wandered into a far country where, in adventure after adventure and sensation after sensation, he sought life. But he never found it; he found only frustration and bewilderment. The farther he moved from his father's house, the closer he came to the house of despair. The more he did what he liked, the less he liked what he did. After the boy had wasted all, a famine developed in the land, and he ended up seeking food in a pig's trough. But the story does not end there. It goes on to say that in this state of disillusionment, blinding frustration and homesickness, the boy "came to himself" and said, "I will arise and go to my father, and will say to him, Father, I have sinned against heaven and before thee." The prodigal son was not himself when he left his father's house or when he dreamed that pleasure was the end of life. Only when he made up his mind to go home and be a son again did he really come to himself. The parable ends with the boy returning home to find a loving father waiting with outstretched arms and heart filled with unutterable joy.

This is an analogy of what America confronts today. Like all human analogies, it is imperfect, but it does suggest some parallels worth considering. America has strayed to the far country of racism and militarism. The home that all too many Americans left was solidly structured idealistically. Its pillars were soundly grounded in the insights of our Judeo-Christian heritage—all men are made in the image of God; all men are brothers; all men are created equal; every man is heir to a legacy of dignity and worth; every man has rights that are neither conferred by nor derived from the state, they are God-given; out of one blood God made all men to dwell upon the face of the earth. What a marvelous foundation for any home! What a glorious and healthy place to inhabit! But America strayed away; and this unnatural excursion has brought only confusion and bewilderment. It has left hearts aching with guilt and minds distorted with irrationality. It has driven wisdom from her sacred throne. This long and callous sojourn in the far country of racism and militarism has brought a moral and spiritual famine to the nation.

It is time for all people of conscience to call upon America to return to her true home of brotherhood and peaceful pursuits. We cannot remain silent as our nation engages in one of history's most cruel and senseless wars. America must continue to have, during these days of human travail, a company of creative dissenters. We need them because the thunder of their fearless voices will be the only sound stronger than the blasts of bombs and the clamour of war hysteria.

Those of us who love peace must organize as effectively as the war hawks. As they spread the propaganda of war we must spread the propaganda of peace. We must combine the fervor of the civil rights movement with the peace movement. We must demonstrate, teach and preach, until the very foundations of our nation are shaken. We must work unceasingly to lift this nation that we love to a higher destiny, to a new plateau of compassion, to a more noble expression of humane-ness.

I have tried to be honest today. To be honest is to confront the truth. To be honest is to realize that the ultimate measure of a man is not where he stands in moments of convenience and moments of comfort, but where he stands in moments of challenge and moments of controversy. However unpleasant and inconvenient the truth may be, I believe we must expose and face it if we are to achieve a better quality of American life.

Just the other day, the distinguished American historian, Henry Steele Commager, told a Senate Committee: "Justice Holmes used to say that the first lesson a judge had to learn was that he was not God ... we do tend perhaps more than other nations, to transform our wars into crusades ... our current involvement in Vietnam is cast, increasingly, into a moral mold ... It is my feeling that we do not have the resources, material, intellectual or moral, to be at once an American power, a European power and an Asian power."

I agree with Mr. Commager. And I would suggest that there is, however, another kind of power that America can and should be. It is a moral power, a power harnessed to the service of peace and human beings, not an inhumane power unleashed against defenseless people. All the world knows that America is a great military power. We need not be diligent in seeking to prove it. We must now show the world our moral power.

There is an element of urgency in our re-directing American power. We are now faced with the fact that tomorrow is today. We are confronted with the fierce urgency of now. In this unfolding conundrum of life and history there is such a thing as being too late. Procrastination is still the thief of time. Life often leaves us standing bare, naked, and dejected with a lost opportunity. The "tide in the affairs of men" does not remain at flood: it ebbs. We may cry out desperately for time to pause in her passage, but time is adamant to every plea and rushes on. Over the bleached bones and jumbled residue of numerous civilizations are written the pathetic words: "Too late." There is an invisible book of life that faithfully records our vigilance or our neglect. "The moving finger writes, and having writ moves on ..." We still have a choice today: nonviolent co-existence or violent co-annihilation. History will record the choice we made. It is still not too late to make the proper choice. If we decide to become a moral power we will be able to transform the jangling discords of this world into a beautiful symphony of brotherhood. If we make the wise decision we will be able to transform our pending cosmic elegy into a creative psalm of peace. This will be a glorious day. In reaching it we can fulfill the noblest of American dreams.

Reflection Questions

1. What are the casualties of the Vietnam War that Dr. King describes?

2. Dr. King states that the physical casualties of the Vietnam War should be enough to make everyone oppose the war. Why do you think it was important to him to detail the casualties of principles and values as well? What effect do you think this tactic might have had on the audience?

3. Dr. King argues that peace cannot be created through the use of war and violence, and he calls for a shift from an arms race to a "peace race." What do you think a "peace race" could look like? What is one concrete action that could be taken to create peace along the lines Dr. King calls for?

4. Name one war that the United States has engaged in since the Vietnam War. Which of the casualties that Dr. King listed might also be true for this more recent war? Explain your reasoning.

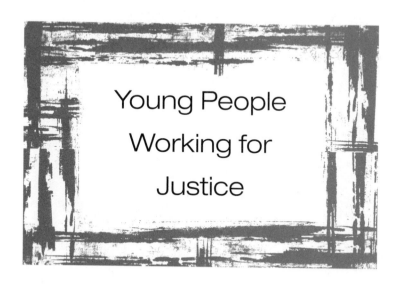

Young People

Working for

Justice

The Time for Freedom
Has Come

In the following article published in the *New York Times Magazine* in 1961, Dr. King cites young people as one of the most significant catalysts in the freedom struggle, applauding the actions of youthful protestors to bring about social change. Dr. King also mentions education as one of the most important tools for empowerment and activism. He commends youth for being ready and willing to draw on their energy and enthusiasm to overcome segregation and injustice.

On a chill morning in the autumn of 1956, an elderly, toilworn Negro woman in Montgomery, Alabama, began her slow, painful four-mile walk to her job. It was the tenth month of the Montgomery bus boycott, which had begun with a life expectancy of one week. The old woman's difficult progress led a passerby to inquire sympathetically if her feet were tired. Her simple answer became the boycotter's watchword. "Yes, friend, my feet is real tired, but my soul is rested."

Five years passed and once more Montgomery arrested the world's attention. Now the symbolic segregationist is not a stubborn, rude bus driver. He emerges in 1961 as a hoodlum stomping the bleeding face of a freedom rider. But neither is the Negro today an elderly woman whose grammar is uncertain; rather, he is college-bred, Ivy League-clad,

---

Originally published in the New York Times Magazine, *September 10, 1961.*

youthful, articulate and resolute. He has the imagination and drive of the young, tamed by discipline and commitment. The nation and the world have reacted with astonishment at these students cast from a new mold, unaware that a chain reaction was accumulating explosive force behind a strangely different façade.

Generating these changes is a phenomenon Victor Hugo described in these words: "There is no greater power on earth than an idea whose time has come." In the decade of the sixties the time for freedom for the Negro has come. This simple truth illuminates the motivations, the tactics and the objectives of the students' daring and imaginative movement.

The young Negro is not in revolt, as some have suggested, against a single pattern of timid, fumbling, conservative leadership. Nor is his conduct to be explained in terms of youth's excesses. He is carrying forward a revolutionary destiny of a whole people consciously and deliberately. Hence the extraordinary willingness to fill the jails as if they were honors classes and the boldness to absorb brutality, even to the point of death, and remain nonviolent. His inner strength derives from his goal of freedom and the leadership role he has grasped even at a time when some of his white counterparts still grope in philosophical confusion searching for a personal goal with human values, searching for security from economic instability, and seeking relief from the haunting fear of nuclear destruction.

The campuses of Negro colleges are infused with a dynamism of both action and philosophical discussion. The needs of a surging period of change have had an impact on all Negro groups, sweeping away conventional trivialities and escapism.

Even in the thirties, when the college campus was alive with social thought, only a minority was involved in action. Now, during the sit-in phase, when a few students were suspended or expelled, more than one college saw the total student body involved in a walkout protest. This is a change in student activity of profound significance. Seldom, if ever, in

American history has a student movement engulfed the whole student body of a college.

In another dimension, an equally striking change is altering the Negro campuses. Not long ago the Negro collegian imitated the white collegian. In attire, in athletics, in social life, imitation was the rule. For the future, he looked to a professional life cast in the image of the middle-class white professional. He imitated with such energy that Gunnar Myrdal described the ambitious Negro as "an exaggerated American."

Today the imitation has ceased. The Negro collegian now initiates. Groping for unique forms of protest, he created the sit-ins and freedom rides. Overnight his white fellow students began to imitate him. As the movement took hold, a revival of social awareness spread across campuses from Cambridge to California. It spilled over the boundaries of the single issue of desegregation and encompassed questions of peace, civil liberties, capital punishment and others. It penetrated the ivy-covered walls of the traditional institutions as well as the glass and stainless-steel structures of the newly-established colleges.

A consciousness of leadership, a sense of destiny have given maturity and dedication to this generation of Negro students which have few precedents. As a minister, I am often given promises of dedication. Instinctively I examine the degree of sincerity. The striking quality in Negro students I have met is the intensity and depth of their commitment. I am no longer surprised to meet attractive, stylishly dressed young girls whose charm and personality would grace a junior prom and to hear them declare in unmistakably sincere terms, "Dr. King, I am ready to die if I must."

Many of the students, when pressed to express their inner feelings, identify themselves with students in Africa, Asia and South America. The liberation struggle in Africa has been the greatest single international influence on American Negro students. Frequently I hear them say that if their African brothers can break the bonds of colonialism, surely the American Negro can break Jim Crow.

African leaders such as President Kwame Nkrumah of Ghana, Governor General Nnamdi Azikiwe of Nigeria, Dr. Tom Mboya of Kenya and Dr. Hastings Banda of Nyasaland are popular heroes on most Negro college campuses. Many groups demonstrated or otherwise protested when the Congo leader, Patrice Lumumba, was assassinated. The newspapers were mistaken when they interpreted these outbursts of indignation as "Communist-inspired."

Part of the impatience of Negro youth stems from their observation that change is taking place rapidly in Africa and other parts of the world, but comparatively slowly in the South. When the United States Supreme Court handed down its historic desegregation decision in 1954, many of us, perhaps naively, thought that great and sweeping school integration would ensue. Yet, today, seven years later, only seven percent of the Negro children of the South have been placed in desegregated schools. At the current rate it will take ninety-three more years to desegregate the public schools of the South. The collegians say, "We can't wait that long" or simply, "We won't wait!"

Negro students are coming to understand that education and learning have become tools for shaping the future and not devices of privilege for an exclusive few. Behind this spiritual explosion is the shattering of a material atom.

The future of the Negro college student has long been locked within the narrow walls of limited opportunity. Only a few professions could be practiced by Negros and, but for a few exceptions, behind barriers of segregation in the North as well as the South. Few frustrations can compare with the experience of struggling with complex academic subjects, straining to absorb concepts which may never be used, or only half-utilized under conditions insulting to the trained mind.

A Negro intern blurted out to me shortly after his patient died, "I wish I were not so well trained because then I would never know how many of these people need not die for lack of proper equipment, adequate post-operative care and timely admission. I'm not practicing good medicine. I'm presiding over tragedies which the absence of good medicine creates."

The Negro lawyer knows his practice will bulk large with criminal cases. The law of wills, of corporations, of taxation will only infrequently reach his office because the clientele he serves has had little opportunity to accumulate property. In his courtroom experience in the South, his clients and witnesses will probably be segregated and he, as well as they, will seldom be referred to as "Mister." Even worse, all too often he knows that the verdict was sealed the moment the arrest was made.

These are but a few examples of the real experience of the Negro professional, seen clearly by the student who has been asked to study with serious purpose. Obviously his incentive has been smothered and weakened. But today, more than ever, the Negro realizes that, while studying, he can also act to change the conditions which cripple his future. In the struggle to desegregate society he is altering it directly for himself as well as for future generations.

There is another respect in which the Negro student is benefiting, and simultaneously contributing to, society as a whole. He is learning social responsibility; he is learning to earn, through his own direct sacrifice, the result he seeks. There are those who would make him soft, pliable and conformist—a mechanical organization man or an uncreative status seeker. But the experience of Negro youth is as harsh and demanding as that of the pioneer on the untamed frontier. Because his struggle is complex, there is no place in it for the frivolous or rowdy. Knowledge and discipline are as indispensable as courage and self-sacrifice. Hence the forging of priceless qualities of character is taking place daily as a high moral goal is pursued.

Inevitably there will emerge from this caldron a mature man, experienced in life's lessons, socially aware, unafraid of experimentation and, most of all, imbued with the spirit of service and dedication to a great ideal. The movement therefore gives to its participants a double education—academic learning from books and classes, and life's lessons from responsible participation in social action. Indeed, the answer to the quest for a more mature, educated American, to compete successfully with the young people of other lands, may be present in this new movement.

Of course, not every student in our struggle has gained from it. This would be more than any humanly designed plan could realize. For some, the opportunity for personal advantage presented itself and their character was not equal to the challenge. A small percentage of students have found it convenient to escape from their own inadequacies by identifying with the sit-ins and other activities. They are, however, relatively few because this is a form of escape in which the flight from responsibility imposes even greater responsibilities and risks.

It is not a solemn life, for all of its seriousness. During a vigorous debate among a group of students discussing the moral and practical soundness of nonviolence, a majority rejected the employment of force. As the minority dwindled to a single student, he finally declared, "All I know is that, if rabbits could throw rocks, there would be fewer hunters in the forest."

This is more than a witty remark to relieve the tensions of serious and even grim discussion. It expresses some of the pent-up impatience, some of the discontent and some of the despair produced by minute corrections in the face of enormous evil. Students necessarily have conflicting reactions. It is understandable that violence presents itself as a quick, effective answer for a few.

For the large majority, however, nonviolent, direct action has emerged as the better and more successful way out. It does not require that they abandon their discontent. This discontent is a sound, healthy social response to the injustice and brutality they see around them. Nonviolence offers a method by which they can fight the evil with which they cannot live. It offers a unique weapon which, without firing a single bullet, disarms the adversary. It exposes his moral defenses, weakens his morale, and at the same time works on his conscience.

Another weapon which Negro students have employed creatively in their nonviolent struggle is satire. It has enabled them to avoid corrosive anger while pressing the cutting edge of ridicule against the opponent. When they have been admonished to "go slow," patiently to wait for gradual change, with a straight face they will assure you that they are diligently searching for the happy medium between the two extremes of moderation and gradualism.

It is perhaps the special quality of nonviolent direct action, which sublimates anger, that explains why so few students are attracted to extreme nationalist sects advocating black supremacy. The students have anger under controlling bonds of discipline. Hence they can answer appeals for cooling-off periods by advocating cooling-off for those who are hot with anger and violence.

Much has been made of the willingness of these devotees of nonviolent social action to break the law. Paradoxically, although they have embraced Thoreau's and Gandhi's civil disobedience on a scale dwarfing any past experience in American history, they do respect law. They feel a moral responsibility to obey just laws. But they recognize that there are also unjust laws.

From a purely moral point of view, an unjust law is one that is out of harmony with the moral law of the universe. More concretely, an unjust law is one in which the minority is compelled to observe a code that is not binding on the majority. An unjust law is one in which people are required to obey a code that they had no part in making because they were denied the right to vote.

In disobeying such unjust laws, the students do so peacefully, openly and nonviolently. Most important, they willingly accept the penalty, whatever it is, for in this way the public comes to reexamine the law in question and will thus decide whether it uplifts or degrades man.

This distinguishes their position on civil disobedience from the "uncivil disobedience" of the segregationist. In the face of laws they consider unjust, the racists seek to defy, evade and circumvent the law, and they are unwilling to accept the penalty. The end result of their defiance is anarchy and disrespect for the law. The students, on the other hand, believe that he who openly disobeys a law, a law conscience tells him is unjust, and then willingly accepts the penalty, gives evidence thereby that he so respects that law that he belongs in jail until it is changed. Their appeal is to the conscience.

Beyond this, the students appear to have perceived what an older generation overlooked in the role of law. The law tends to declare rights—it does not deliver them. A catalyst is needed to breathe life experience into a judicial decision by the persistent exercise of the rights until they become usual and ordinary in human conduct. They have offered their energies, their bodies to effect this result. They see themselves the obstetricians at the birth of a new order. It is in this manner that the students have related themselves to and materialized "the idea whose time has come."

In a sense, the victories of the past two years have been spectacular and considerable. Because of the student sitters, more than 150 cities in the South have integrated their lunch counters. Actually, the current breakthroughs have come about partly as a result of the patient legal, civil and social ground clearing of the previous decades. Then, too, but slowly, the national government is realizing that our so-called domestic race relations are a major force in our foreign relations. Our image abroad reflects our behavior at home.

Many liberals, of the North as well as the South, when they list the unprecedented programs of the past few years, yearn for a "cooling-off" period; not too fast, they say, we may lose all that we have gained if we push faster than the violent ones can be persuaded to yield.

This view, though understandable, is a misreading of the goals of the young Negroes. They are not after "mere tokens" of integration ("tokenism," they call it); rather theirs is a revolt against the whole system of Jim Crow and they are prepared to sit-in, kneel-in, wade-in and stand-in until every waiting room, rest room, theatre and other facility throughout the nation that is supposedly open to the public is in fact open to Negroes, Mexicans, Indians, Jews or what have you. Theirs is total commitment to this goal of equality and dignity. And for this achievement they are prepared to pay the costs—whatever they are—in suffering and hardship as long as may be necessary.

Indeed, these students are not struggling for themselves alone. They are seeking to save the soul of America. They are taking our whole nation back to those great wells of democracy which were dug deep by the Founding Fathers in the formulation of the Constitution and the Declaration of Independence. In sitting down at the lunch counters, they are in reality standing up for the best in the American dream. They courageously go to the jails of the South in order to get America out of the dilemma in which she finds herself as a result of the continued existence of segregation. One day historians will record this student movement as one of the most significant epics of our heritage.

But should we, as a nation, sit by as spectators when the social unrest seethes? Most of us recognize that the Jim Crow system is doomed. If so, would it not be the wise and human thing to abolish the system surely and swiftly? This would not be difficult, if our national government would exercise its full powers to enforce federal laws and court decisions and do so on a scale commensurate with the problems and with an unmistakable decisiveness. Moreover, we would need our religious, civic and economic leaders to mobilize their forces behind a real, honest-to-goodness "End Jim Crow Now" campaign.

This is the challenge of these young people to us and our ideals. It is also an expression of their new-found faith in themselves as well as in their fellow man.

In an effort to understand the students and to help them understand themselves, I asked one student I know to find a quotation expressing his feeling of our struggle. He was an inarticulate young man, athletically expert and far more poetic with a basketball than with words, but few would have found the quotation he typed on a card and left on my desk early one morning:

> *I sought my soul, but my soul I could not see,*
> *I sought my God, but he eluded me,*
> *I sought my brother, and I found all three.*

Reflection Questions

1. Dr. King refers to young people as "catalysts." Why does Dr. King find such inspiration in young people? What power do young people bring to the freedom movement?

2. What does Dr. King mean when he states, "But today, more than ever, the Negro realizes that, while studying, he can also act to change the conditions which cripple his future. In the struggle to desegregate society he is altering it directly for himself as well as for future generations"?

3. Discuss how American young people's identification with larger freedom struggles in Africa, Asia, and South America fueled their demands and desires for change in the United States. What was the significance of this greater sense of awareness about ending segregation?

4. How does Dr. King define an unjust law? Do you agree with the concept of refusing to follow unjust laws and willingly facing the punishment? Why or why not? Provide an example of an unjust law today.

The Burning Truth in the South

The following article in the *Progressive* magazine appeared at a time when students throughout the South were engaged in sit-ins to end the segregation of lunch counters in that region. Dr. King commends their tenacity and also reminds the reader of the importance of student involvement within the movement. He frames the student protests both within a historical perspective and within the context of the practice of nonviolent direct action.

An electrifying movement of Negro students has shattered the placid surface of campuses and communities across the South. Though confronted in many places by hoodlums, police guns, tear gas, arrests, and jail sentences, the students tenaciously continue to sit down and demand equal service at variety store lunch counters, and extend their protest from city to city. In communities like Montgomery, Alabama, the whole student body rallied behind expelled students and staged a walkout while state government intimidation was unleashed with a display of military force appropriate to a wartime invasion. Nevertheless, the spirit of self-sacrifice and commitment remains firm, and the state governments find themselves dealing with students who have lost the fear of jail and physical injury.

It is no overstatement to characterize these events as historic. Never before in the United States has so large a body of students spread a

Originally published in the Progressive *(May 1960).*

struggle over so great an area in pursuit of a goal of human dignity and freedom.

The suddenness with which this development burst upon the nation has given rise to the description "spontaneous." Yet it is not without clearly perceivable causes and precedents. First, we should go back to the ending of World War II. Then, the new will and determination of the Negro were irrevocably generated. Hundreds of thousands of young Negro men were mustered out of the armed forces, and with their honorable discharge papers and GI Bill of Rights grants, they received a promise from a grateful nation that the broader democracy for which they had fought would begin to assume reality. They believed in this promise and acted in the conviction that changes were guaranteed. Some changes did appear—but commensurate neither with the promise nor the need.

Struggles of a local character began to emerge, but the scope and results were limited. Few Americans outside the immediately affected areas even realized a struggle was taking place. One perceptible aspect was the steady, significant increase in voting registration which took place, symbolizing the determination of the Negro, particularly the veteran, to make his rights a reality. The number of registered voters reached a point higher than exists today.

The United States Supreme Court decision of 1954 was viewed by Negroes as the delivery of part of the promise of change. In unequivocal language the Court affirmed that "separate but equal" facilities are inherently unequal, and that to segregate a child on the basis of his race is to deny that child equal protection of the law. This decision brought hope to millions of disinherited Negroes who had formerly dared only to dream of freedom. But the implementation of the decision was not to be realized without a sharp and difficult struggle. Through five years of turmoil some advances were achieved. The victory is far from complete, but the determination by Negroes that it will be won is universal.

What relation have these events to the student sit-downs? It was the young veteran who gave the first surge of power to the postwar civil rights movements. It was the high school, college, and elementary school young people who were in the front line of the school desegregation struggle. Lest it be forgotten, the opening of hundreds of schools to Negroes for the first time in history required that there be young Negroes with the moral and physical courage to face the challenges and, all too frequently, the mortal danger presented by mob resistance.

There were such young Negroes in the tens of thousands, and no program for integration failed for want of students. The simple courage of students and their parents should never be forgotten. In the years 1958 and 1959 two massive Youth Marches to Washington for Integrated Schools involved some forty thousand young people who brought with them nearly five hundred thousand signatures on petitions gathered largely from campuses and youth centers. This mass action infused a new spirit of direct action challenging government to act forthrightly.

Hence for a decade young Negroes have been steeled by both deeds and inspiration to step into responsible action. These are the precedents for the student struggle of today.

Many related, interacting social forces must be understood if we are to understand history as it is being made. The arresting upsurge of Africa and Asia is remote neither in time nor in space to the Negro of the South. Indeed, the determination of Negro Americans to win freedom from all forms of oppression springs from the same deep longing that motivates oppressed peoples all over the world.

However inadequate forms of education and communication may be, the ordinary Negro Jim Smith knows that in primitive jungle villages in India still illiterate peasants are casting a free ballot for their state and federal legislators. In one after another of the new African states black men form the government, write the laws, and administer the affairs of state. But in state after state in the United States the Negro is ruled and governed without a fragment of participation in civic life. The contrast is a burning truth which has molded a deep determination to end this intolerable condition.

Negroes have also experienced sharp frustrations as they struggle for the realization of promises expressed in hollow legislative enactments or empty electoral campaign oratory. Conferences from the lowest levels of officialdom up to the Chief Executive in the White House result in the clarification of problems—but not their solution. Studies by many commissions, unhappily devoid of power, continue to pose problems without any concrete results that could be translated into jobs, education, equality of opportunity, and access to the fruits of an historic period of prosperity. In "the affluent society," the Negro has remained the poor, the underprivileged, and the lowest class. Court actions are often surrounded by a special type of red tape that has made for long drawn-out processes of litigation and evasive schemes. The Negro has also become aware that token integration was not a start in good faith but a new form of discrimination covered up with certain niceties.

It was inevitable, therefore, that a more direct approach would be sought—one which would contain the promise of some immediate degree of success based upon the concrete act of the Negro. Hence, a period began in which the emphasis shifted from the slow court process to direct action in the form of bus protests, economic boycotts, mass marches to and demonstrations in the nation's capital and state capitals.

One may wonder why the present movement started with the lunch counters. The answer lies in the fact that here the Negro has suffered indignities and injustices that cannot be justified or explained. Almost every Negro has experienced the tragic inconveniences of lunch counter segregation. He cannot understand why he is welcomed with open arms at most counters in the store, but is denied service at a certain counter because it happens to be selling food and drink. In a real sense the "sit-ins" represent more than a demand for service; they represent a demand for respect.

It is absurd to think of this movement as being initiated by Communists or some other outside group. This movement is an expression of the longing of a new Negro for freedom and human dignity. These students were anchored to lunch counter seats by the accumulated indignities of days gone by and the boundless aspirations of generations yet unborn.

In this new method of protest a new philosophy provided a special undergirding—the philosophy of nonviolence. It was first modestly and quietly projected in one community, Montgomery, when the threat of violence became real in the bus protest. But it burst from this limited arena, and was embraced by masses of people across the nation with fervor and consistency.

The appeal of nonviolence has many facets:

First—It proclaims the sincere and earnest wish of the Negro that though changes must be accomplished, there is no desire to use or tolerate force. Thus, it is consistent with the deeply religious traditions of Negroes.

Second—It denies that vengeance for past oppression motivates the new spirit of determined struggle.

Third—It brings to the point of action a great multitude who need the assurance that a technique exists which is suitable and practical for a minority confronting a majority often vicious and possessed of effective weapons of combat.

Fourth—Many Negroes recognize the necessity of creating discord to alter established community patterns, but they strongly desire that controls be built [in], so that neither they nor their adversaries would find themselves engaged in mutual destruction.

Fifth—Having faith that the white majority is not an undifferentiated whole, Negro leaders have welcomed a moral appeal which can reach the emotions and intellect of significant white groups.

The appeal of the philosophy of nonviolence encompasses these many requirements. The key significance of the student movement lies in the fact that from its inception, everywhere, it has combined direct action [and] nonviolence.

This quality has given it the extraordinary power and discipline which every thinking person observes. It has discredited the adversary, who knows how to deal with force but is bewildered and panicky in the face of the new techniques. Time will reveal that the students are learning lessons not contained in their textbooks. Hundreds have already been expelled, fined, imprisoned, and brutalized, and the numbers continue to grow. But with the punishments, something more is growing. A generation of young people has come out of decades of shadows to face naked state power; it has lost its fears, and experienced the majestic dignity of a direct struggle for its own liberation. These young people have connected up with their own history—the slave revolts, the incomplete revolution of the Civil War, the brotherhood of colonial colored men in Africa and Asia. They are an integral part of the history which is reshaping the world, replacing a dying order with modern democracy. They are doing this in a nation whose own birth spread new principles and shattered a medieval social society then dominating most of the globe.

It is extremely significant that in many places the Negro students have found white allies to join in their actions. It is equally significant that on a mass scale students and adults in the North and elsewhere have organized supporting actions, many of which are still only in their early stages.

The segregationists now face some hard alternatives: They can continue to seek to maintain segregated facilities. In this event they must live with discord or themselves initiate, and be responsible for, violence with all its evil consequences. They may close the facilities as they have done in many places. But this will not end the movement; rather, it will spread to libraries, public parks, schools, and the like, and these too will have to be closed, thus depriving both white and Negro of necessary cultural and recreational institutions. This would be a step backward for the whole of society. Or finally, they can accept the principle of equality. In this case they still have two alternative approaches. They may make the facilities equally bad for both white and Negro or equally good. Thus finally the simple logic and justice in their own interests should direct them to the only acceptable solution—to accept equality and maintain it on the best level for both races.

The outcome of the present struggle will be some time in unfolding, but the line of its direction is clear. It is a final refutation of the time-honored theory that the Negro prefers segregation. It would be futile to deplore, as many do, the tensions accompanying the social changes. Tension and conflict are not alien nor abnormal to growth but are the natural results of the process of changes. A revolution is occurring in both the social order and the human mind. One hundred eighty-four years ago a bold group of men signed the Declaration of Independence. If their struggle had been lost they had signed their own death warrant. Nevertheless, though explicitly regretting that King George had forced them to this extreme by a long "train of abuses," they resolutely acted and a great new society was born. The Negro students, their parents, and their allies are acting today in that imperishable tradition.

Reflection Questions

1. Dr. King argues that young people did not spontaneously decide to protest. What were the historical events that led up to college students' protests? How did the students' protests build on what had come before?

2. What is a lunch counter and where were they located? Why were the lunch counters such an important place of protest?

3. Dr. King writes, "It is extremely significant that in many places the Negro students have found white allies to join in their actions." Why do you think this was so significant? What effects do you think it might have had on the protests?

4. Name a group of young people fighting against oppression or inequality today.

Black and White Together

Faced with diminishing adult support for protests in Birmingham, in 1963 Dr. King turned to the city's young people. James Bevel of the Southern Christian Leadership Conference (SCLC) suggested recruiting local students to participate, reasoning that since they did not have jobs to lose, they would be more willing to risk arrest. After being trained in the principles of nonviolence, more than one thousand African American students skipped their classes on May 2 and gathered in downtown Birmingham, marching directly into police lines to demand desegregation of local businesses, public facilities and restaurants. While hundreds were arrested and jailed, many more young people returned the next day to take their places. In the ensuing confrontation, T. Eugene "Bull" Connor, Birmingham's commissioner of public safety, ordered fire hoses and police dogs to be unleashed on the unarmed protestors. Here, Dr. King recounts the "Children's Crusade" and other important events that led to the end of segregation in Birmingham.

After eight days of imprisonment, Ralph Abernathy and I accepted bond to come out of jail for two purposes. It was necessary for me to regain communication with the S.C.L.C. officers and our lawyers in order to map the strategy for the contempt cases that

From Why We Can't Wait *(Harper & Row, 1963, 1964,
reprinted by Beacon Press, 2010).*

would be coming up shortly in the circuit court. Also, I had decided to put into operation a new phase of our campaign, which I felt would speed victory.

I called my staff together and repeated a conviction I had been voicing ever since the campaign began. If our drive was to be successful, we must involve the students of the community. In most of the recent direct-action crusades, it had been the young people who sparked the movement. But in Birmingham, of the first four or five hundred people who had submitted themselves to arrest, two-thirds had been adults. We had considered this a good thing at the time, for a really effective campaign incorporates a cross section of the community. But now it was time to enlist the young people in larger numbers. Even though we realized that involving teenagers and high-school students would bring down upon us a heavy fire of criticism, we felt that we needed this dramatic new dimension. Our people were demonstrating daily and going to jail in numbers, but we were still beating our heads against the brick wall of the city officials' stubborn resolve to maintain the status quo. Our fight, if won, would benefit people of all ages. But most of all we were inspired with a desire to give to our young a true sense of their own stake in freedom and justice. We believed they would have the courage to respond to our call.

James Bevel, Andy Young, Bernard Lee and Dorothy Cotton began visiting colleges and high schools in the area. They invited students to attend after-school meetings at churches. The word spread fast, and the response from Birmingham's youngsters exceeded our fondest dreams. By the fifties and by the hundreds, these youngsters attended mass meetings and training sessions. They listened eagerly as we talked of bringing freedom to Birmingham, not in some distant time, but right now. We taught them the philosophy of nonviolence. We challenged them to bring their exuberance, their youthful creativity, into the disciplined dedication of the movement. We found them eager to belong, hungry for participation in a significant social effort. Looking back, it is clear that the introduction of Birmingham's children into the campaign was one of the wisest moves we made. It brought a new impact to the crusade, and the impetus that we needed to win the struggle.

Immediately, of course, a cry of protest went up. Although by the end of April the attitude of the national press had changed considerably, so that the major media were according us sympathetic coverage, yet many deplored our "using" our children in this fashion. Where had these writers been, we wondered, during the centuries when our segregated social system had been misusing and abusing Negro children? Where had they been with their protective words when, down through the years, Negro infants were born into ghettos, taking their first breath of life in a social atmosphere where the fresh air of freedom was crowded out by the stench of discrimination?

The children themselves had the answer to the misguided sympathies of the press. One of the most ringing replies came from a child of no more than eight who walked with her mother one day in a demonstration. An amused policeman leaned down to her and said with mock gruffness: "What do you want?"

The child looked into his eyes, unafraid, and gave her answer.

"F'eedom," she said.

She could not even pronounce the word, but no Gabriel trumpet could have sounded a truer note.

Even children too young to march requested and earned a place in our ranks. Once when we sent out a call for volunteers, six tiny youngsters responded. Andy Young told them that they were not old enough to go to jail but that they could go to the library. "You won't get arrested there," he said, "but you might learn something." So these six small children marched off to the building in the white district, where, up to two weeks before, they would have been turned away at the door. Shyly but doggedly, they went to the children's room and sat down, and soon they were lost in their books. In their own way, they had struck a blow, for freedom.

The children understood the stakes they were fighting for. I think of one teenage boy whose father's devotion to the movement turned sour when he learned that his son had pledged himself to become a demonstrator. The father forbade his son to participate.

"Daddy," the boy said, "I don't want to disobey you, but I have made my pledge. If you try to keep me home, I will sneak off. If you think I deserve to be punished for that, I'll just have to take the punishment. For, you see, I'm not doing this only because I want to be free. I'm doing it also because I want freedom for you and Mama, and I want it to come before you die."

That father thought again, and gave his son his blessing.

The movement was blessed by the fire and excitement brought to it by young people such as these. And when Birmingham youngsters joined the march in numbers, an historic thing happened. For the first time in the civil-rights movement, we were able to put into effect the Gandhian principle: "Fill up the jails."

Jim Bevel had the inspiration of setting a "D" Day, when the students would go to jail in historic numbers. When that day arrived, young people converged on the Sixteenth Street Baptist Church in wave after wave. Altogether on "D" Day, May 2, more than a thousand young people demonstrated and went to jail. At one school, the principal gave orders to lock the gates to keep the students in. The youngsters climbed over the gates and ran toward freedom. The assistant superintendent of schools threatened them with expulsion, and still they came, day after day. At the height of the campaign, by conservative estimates, there were 2,500 demonstrators in jail at one time, a large proportion of them young people.

Serious as they were about what they were doing, these teenagers had that marvelous humor that arms the unarmed in the face of danger. Under their leaders, they took delight in confusing the police. A small decoy group would gather at one exit of the church, bringing policemen streaming in cars and on motorcycles. Before the officers knew what was happening, other groups, by the scores, would pour out of other exits and move, two by two, toward our goal in the downtown section.

Many arrived at their destination before the police could confront and arrest them. They sang as they marched and as they were loaded into the paddy wagons. The police ran out of paddy wagons and had to press sheriff's cars and school buses into service.

Watching those youngsters in Birmingham, I could not help remembering an episode in Montgomery during the bus boycott. Someone had asked an elderly woman why she was involved in our struggle.

"I'm doing it for my children and for my grandchildren," she had replied.

Seven years later, the children and grandchildren were doing it for themselves.

II

With the jails filling up and the scorching glare of national disapproval focused on Birmingham, Bull Connor abandoned his posture of nonviolence. The result was an ugliness too well known to Americans and to people all over the world. The newspapers of May 4 carried pictures of prostrate women, and policemen bending over them with raised clubs; of children marching up to the bared fangs of police dogs; of the terrible force of pressure hoses sweeping bodies into the streets.

This was the time of our greatest stress, and the courage and conviction of those students and adults made it our finest hour. We did not fight back, but we did not turn back. We did not give way to bitterness. Some few spectators, who had not been trained in the discipline of nonviolence, reacted to the brutality of the policemen by throwing rocks and bottles. But the demonstrators remained nonviolent. In the face of this resolution and bravery, the moral conscience of the nation was deeply stirred and, all over the country, our fight became the fight of decent Americans of all races and creeds.

The moral indignation which was spreading throughout the land; the sympathy created by the children; the growing involvement of the

Negro community—all these factors were mingling to create a certain atmosphere inside our movement. It was a pride in progress and a conviction that we were going to win. It was a mounting optimism which gave us the feeling that the implacable barriers that confronted us were doomed and already beginning to crumble. We were advised, in the utmost confidence, that the white business structure was weakening under the adverse publicity, the pressure of our boycott, and a parallel falling-off of white buying.

Strangely enough, the masses of white citizens in Birmingham were not fighting us. This was one of the most amazing aspects of the Birmingham crusade. Only a year or so ago, had we begun such a campaign, Bull Connor would have had his job done for him by murderously angry white citizens. Now, however, the majority were maintaining a strictly hands-off policy. I do not mean to insinuate that they were in sympathy with our cause or that they boycotted stores because we did. I simply suggest that it is powerfully symbolic of shifting attitudes in the South that the majority of the white citizens of Birmingham remained neutral through our campaign. This neutrality added force to our feeling that we were on the road to victory.

On one dramatic occasion even Bull Connor's men were shaken. It was a Sunday afternoon, when several hundred Birmingham Negroes had determined to hold a prayer meeting near the city jail. They gathered at the New Pilgrim Baptist Church and began an orderly march. Bull Connor ordered out the police dogs and fire hoses. When the marchers approached the border between the white and Negro areas, Connor ordered them to turn back. The Reverend Charles Billups, who was leading the march, politely refused. Enraged, Bull Connor whirled on his men and shouted:

"Dammit. Turn on the hoses."

What happened in the next thirty seconds was one of the most fantastic events of the Birmingham story. Bull Connor's men, their deadly hoses poised for action, stood facing the marchers. The marchers, many of them on their knees, stared back, unafraid and unmoving. Slowly the Negroes stood up and began to advance. Connor's men, as though hypnotized, fell back, their hoses sagging uselessly in their hands while several hundred Negroes marched past them, without further interference, and held their prayer meeting as planned.

One more factor helped to encourage us in the belief that our goals were coming within reach. We had demonstrated in defiance of a civil injunction. For this act of disobedience, we had been cited for contempt. In Alabama, if you are cited for criminal contempt, you serve five days and that is the end of it. If you are cited for civil contempt, however, you figuratively hold the jailhouse keys in the palm of your hand. At any time, if you are willing to recant, you can earn release. If you do not recant, you can be held for the rest of your natural life.

Most of the demonstrators had been cited for criminal contempt. About ten of us, however, all leaders of the movement, had been cited for civil contempt. When we were first placed under this charge, I am certain that the Birmingham authorities believed we would back down rather than face the threat of indefinite imprisonment. But by the time we appeared in court late in April to answer the charges, all of Birmingham knew that we would never recant, even if we had to rot away in their jails. The city thus faced the prospect of putting us into jail for life. Confronted with the certain knowledge that we would not give in, the city attorney undoubtedly realized that he would be sentencing us to a martyrdom which must eventually turn the full force of national public opinion against Birmingham.

Abruptly the tactics were reversed. The civil-contempt charge was changed to the less stringent criminal-contempt charge, under which we were swiftly convicted on April 26. In addition, the judge announced that he would delay sentence and give us about twenty days to file an appeal. At this point there was little doubt in our minds that Birmingham's bastions of segregation were weakening.

III

Throughout the campaign, we had been seeking to establish some dialogue with the city leaders in an effort to negotiate on four major issues:

1. The desegregation of lunch counters, restrooms, fitting rooms and drinking fountains in variety and department stores.

2. The upgrading and hiring of Negroes on a non-discriminatory basis throughout the business and industrial community of Birmingham.

3. The dropping of all charges against jailed demonstrators.

4. The creation of a biracial committee to work out a timetable for desegregation in other areas of Birmingham life.

Even though pressure on Birmingham's business community was intense, there were stubborn men in its midst who seemed to feel they would rather see their own enterprises fail than sit across the table and negotiate with our leadership. However, when national pressure began to pile up on the White House, climaxing with the infamous day of May 3, the administration was forced to act. On May 4, the attorney general dispatched Burke Marshall, his chief civil-rights assistant, and Joseph F. Dolan, assistant deputy attorney general, to seek a truce in the tense racial situation. Though Marshall had no ultimate power to impose a solution, he had full authority to represent the president in the negotiations. It was one of the first times the federal government had taken so active a role in such circumstances.

I must confess that although I appreciated the fact that the administration had finally made a decisive move, I had some initial misgivings concerning Marshall's intentions. I was afraid that he had come to urge a "cooling off" period—to ask us to declare a one-sided truce as a condition to negotiations. To his credit, Marshall did not adopt such a position. Rather, he did an invaluable job of opening channels of communication between our leadership and the top people in the economic power structure. Said one staunch defender of segregation, after conferring with Marshall: "There is a man who listens. I had to listen back, and I guess I grew up a little."

With Burke Marshall as catalyst, we began to hold secret meetings with the Senior Citizens Committee. At these sessions, unpromising as they were at the outset, we laid the groundwork for the agreement that would eventually accord us all of our major demands.

Meanwhile, however, for several days violence swept through the streets of Birmingham. An armored car was added to Bull Connor's strange armament. And some Negroes, not trained in our nonviolent methods, again responded with bricks and bottles. On one of these days, when the pressure in Connor's hoses was so high that it peeled the bark off the trees, Fred Shuttlesworth was hurled by a blast of water against the side of a building. Suffering injuries in his chest, he was carried away in an ambulance. Connor, when told, responded in characteristic fashion. "I wish he'd been carried away in a hearse," he said. Fortunately, Shuttlesworth is resilient and though still in pain he was back at the conference table the next day.

Terrified by the very destructiveness brought on by their own acts, the city police appealed for state troopers to be brought into the area. Many of the white leaders now realized that something had to be done. Yet there were those among them who were still adamant. But one other incident was to occur that would transform recalcitrance into good faith. On Tuesday, May 7, the Senior Citizens Committee had assembled in a downtown building to discuss our demands. In the first hours of this meeting, they were so intransigent that Burke Marshall despaired of a pact. The atmosphere was charged with tension, and tempers were running high.

In this mood, these 125-odd business leaders adjourned for lunch. As they walked out on the street, an extraordinary sight met their eyes.

On that day several thousand Negroes had marched on the town. The jails were so full that the police could only arrest a handful. There were Negroes on the sidewalks, in the streets, standing, sitting in the aisles of downtown stores. There were square blocks of Negroes, a veritable sea of black faces. They were committing no violence; they were just present and singing. Downtown Birmingham echoed to the strains of the freedom songs.

Astounded, those businessmen, key figures in a great city, suddenly realized that the movement could not be stopped. When they returned—from the lunch they were unable to get—one of the men who had been in the most determined opposition cleared his throat and said: "You know, I've been thinking this thing through. We ought to be able to work something out."

That admission marked the beginning of the end. Late that afternoon, Burke Marshall informed us that representatives from the business and industrial community wanted to meet with the movement leaders immediately to work out a settlement. After talking with these men for about three hours, we became convinced that they were negotiating in good faith. On the basis of this assurance we called a twenty-four-hour truce on Wednesday morning.

That day the president devoted the entire opening statement of his press conference to the Birmingham situation, emphasizing how vital it was that the problems be squarely faced and resolved and expressing encouragement that a dialogue now existed between the opposing sides. Even while the president spoke, the truce was briefly threatened when Ralph and I were suddenly clapped into jail on an old charge. Some of my associates, feeling that they had again been betrayed, put on their walking shoes and prepared to march. They were restrained, however; we were swiftly bailed out; and negotiations were resumed.

After talking all night Wednesday, and practically all day and night Thursday, we reached an accord. On Friday, May 10, this agreement was announced. It contained the following pledges:

1. The desegregation of lunch counters, restrooms, fitting rooms and drinking fountains, in planned stages within ninety days after signing.

2. The upgrading and hiring of Negroes on a non-discriminatory basis throughout the industrial community of Birmingham, to include [the] hiring of Negroes as clerks and salesmen within sixty days after signing of the agreement—and the immediate appointment of a committee of business, industrial and professional leaders to implement an area-wide program for the acceleration of upgrading and employment of Negroes in job categories previously denied to them.

3. Official cooperation with the movement's legal representatives in working out the release of all jailed persons on bond or on their personal recognizance.

4. Through the Senior Citizens Committee or Chamber of Commerce, communications between Negro and white to be publicly established within two weeks after signing, in order to prevent the necessity of further demonstrations and protests.

Our troubles were not over. The announcement that a peace pact had been signed in Birmingham was flashed across the world by the hundred-odd foreign correspondents then covering the campaign on the crowded scene. It was headlined in the nation's press and heralded on network television. Segregationist forces within the city were consumed with fury. They vowed reprisals against the white businessmen who had "betrayed" them by capitulating to the cause of Negro equality. On Saturday night, they gave their brutal answer to the pact. Following a Ku Klux Klan meeting on the outskirts of town, the home of my brother, the Reverend A. D. King, was bombed. That same night a bomb was planted near the Gaston Motel, a bomb so placed as to kill or seriously wound anyone who might have been in Room 30—my room. Evidently the would-be assassins did not know I was in Atlanta that night.

The bombing had been well timed. The bars in the Negro district close at midnight, and the bombs exploded just as some of Birmingham's Saturday-night drinkers came out of the bars. Thousands of Negroes poured into the streets. Wyatt Walker, my brother and others urged them to go home, but they were not under the discipline of the movement and were in no mood to listen to counsels of peace. Fighting began. Stones were hurled at the police. Cars were wrecked and fires started. Whoever planted the bombs had *wanted* the Negroes to riot. They wanted the pact upset.

Governor George Wallace's state police and "conservation men" sealed off the Negro area and moved in with their bullies and pistols. They beat numerous innocent Negroes; among their acts of chivalry was the clubbing of the diminutive Anne Walker, Wyatt's wife, as she was about to enter her husband's quarters at the partially bombed-out Gaston Motel. They further distinguished themselves by beating Wyatt when he was attempting to drive back home after seeing his wife to the hospital.

I shall never forget the phone call my brother placed to me in Atlanta that violent Saturday night. His home had just been destroyed. Several people had been injured at the motel. I listened as he described the erupting tumult and catastrophe in the streets of the city. Then, in the background as he talked, I heard a swelling burst of beautiful song. Feet planted in the rubble of debris, threatened by criminal violence and hatred, followers of the movement were singing "We Shall Overcome." I marveled that in a moment of such tragedy the Negro could still express himself with hope and with faith.

The following evening, a thoroughly aroused president told the nation that the federal government would not allow extremists to sabotage a fair and just pact. He ordered three thousand federal troops into position near Birmingham and made preparations to federalize the Alabama National Guard. This firm action stopped the troublemakers in their tracks.

Yet the segregationist die-hards were to attempt still once more to destroy the peace. On May 20 the headlines announced that more than a thousand students who had participated in the demonstrations had been either suspended or expelled by the city's Board of Education. I am convinced that this was another attempt to drive the Negro community to an unwise and impulsive move. The plot might have worked; there were some people in our ranks who sincerely felt that, in retaliation, all the students of Birmingham should stay out of school and that demonstrations should be resumed.

I was out of the city at the time, but I rushed back to Birmingham to persuade the leaders that we must not fall into the trap. We decided to take the issue into the courts and did so, through the auspices of the N.A.A.C.P. Legal Defense and Educational Fund. On May 22, the local federal district judge upheld the Birmingham Board of Education. But that same day, Judge Elbert P. Tuttle, of the Fifth Circuit Court of Appeals, not only reversed the decision of the district judge but strongly condemned the Board of Education for its action. In a time when the nation is trying to solve the problem of school drop-outs, Judge Tuttle's ruling indicated, it is an act of irresponsibility to drive those youngsters from school in retaliation for having engaged in legally permissible action to achieve their constitutional rights. The night this ruling was handed down, we had a great mass meeting. It was a jubilant moment, another victory in the titanic struggle.

The following day, in an appropriate postscript, the Alabama Supreme Court ruled Eugene "Bull" Connor and his fellow commissioners out of office, once and for all.

IV

I could not close an account of events in Birmingham without noting the tremendous moral and financial support which poured in upon us from all over the world during the six weeks of demonstrations and in the weeks and months to follow. Although we were so preoccupied with the day-to-day crises of the campaign that we did not have time to send out a formal plea for funds, letters of encouragement and donations ranging from pennies taken from piggy banks to checks of impressive size flowed into our besieged command post at the Gaston Motel and our Atlanta headquarters.

One of the most gratifying developments was the unprecedented show of unity that was displayed by the national Negro community in support of our crusade. From all over the country came Negro ministers, civil-rights leaders, entertainers, star athletes and ordinary citizens, ready to speak at our meetings or join us in jail. The N.A.A.C.P. Legal Defense and Educational Fund came to our aid several times both with money and with resourceful legal talent. Many other organizations and individuals contributed invaluable gifts of time, money and moral support.

The signing of the agreement was the climax of a long struggle for justice, freedom and human dignity. The millennium still had not come, but Birmingham had made a fresh, bold step toward equality. Today Birmingham is by no means miraculously desegregated. There is still resistance and violence. The last-ditch struggle of a segregationist governor still soils the pages of current events and it is still necessary for a harried president to invoke his highest powers so that a Negro child may go to school with a white child in Birmingham. But these factors only serve to emphasize the truth that even the segregationists know: The system to which they have been committed lies on its deathbed. The only imponderable is the question of how costly they will make the funeral.

I like to believe that Birmingham will one day become a model in southern race relations. I like to believe that the negative extremes of Birmingham's past will resolve into the positive and Utopian extreme of her future; that the sins of a dark yesterday will be redeemed in the achievements of a bright tomorrow. I have this hope because, once on a summer day, a dream came true. The city of Birmingham discovered a conscience.

Reflection Questions

1. What does "freedom" mean when Dr. King and others use it in the context of the freedom movement? What freedom were black people demanding?

2. Dr. King was initially chastised for "using" children in the movement. Do you agree with this accusation? What do you see as the importance in involving children and teenagers?

3. How did the movement change once children and teenagers were involved? Fifty years after the Birmingham Children's Crusade, what is the legacy of the actions of these young people?

4. Trace the evolution of the agreement to desegregate lunch counters throughout this essay, paying attention to interventions by political leaders and others. Which event do you think was most pivotal to the eventual desegregation? Defend your decision.

The Power
of Freedom

Speech at the Great March on Detroit

Originally called the "American Dream" speech, Dr. King delivered various versions of the following speech before giving its most famous iteration, the "I Have a Dream" speech, at the March on Washington. On June 23, 1963, while on a tour that took him from California to New York, Dr. King joined more than 150,000 marchers in the Great March on Detroit. The march ended in Cobo Hall, where King told an audience of about twenty-five thousand about his "dream deeply rooted in the American dream." Two months later, when Dr. King spoke at the Washington march, he would recall the audience's enthusiastic response to his dream refrain.

My good friend, the Reverend C. L. Franklin, all of the officers and members of the Detroit Council of Human Rights, distinguished platform guests, ladies and gentlemen, I cannot begin to say to you this afternoon how thrilled I am, and I cannot begin to tell you the deep joy that comes to my heart as I participate with you in what I consider the largest and greatest demonstration for freedom ever held in the United States. And I can assure you that what has been

Delivered at the Great March on Detroit, Cobo Hall, Detroit, Michigan, June 23, 1963.

done here today will serve as a source of inspiration for all of the free-dom-loving people of this nation.

I think there is something else that must be said because it is a magnificent demonstration of discipline. With all of the thousands and hundreds of thousands of people engaged in this demonstration today, there has not been one reported incident of violence. I think this is a magnificent demonstration of our commitment to nonviolence in this struggle for freedom all over the United States, and I want to commend the leadership of this community for making this great event possible and [*Applause*] through such disciplined channels.

Almost one hundred and one years ago, on September the 22nd, 1862, to be exact, a great and noble American, Abraham Lincoln, signed an executive order, which was to take effect on January the first, 1863. This executive order was called the Emancipation Proclamation and it served to free the Negro from the bondage of physical slavery. But one hundred years later, the Negro in the United States of America still isn't free.

But now more than ever before, America is forced to grapple with this problem, for the shape of the world today does not afford us the luxury of an anemic democracy. The price that this nation must pay for the continued oppression and exploitation of the Negro or any other minority group is the price of its own destruction. For the hour is late. The clock of destiny is ticking out, and we must act now before it is too late.

The events of Birmingham, Alabama, and the more than sixty communities that have started protest movements since Birmingham, are indicative of the fact that the Negro is now determined to be free. For Birmingham tells us something in glaring terms. It says first that the Negro is no longer willing to accept racial segregation in any of its dimensions. For we have come to see that segregation is not only sociologically untenable, it is not only politically unsound, it is morally wrong and sinful. Segregation is a cancer in the body politic, which must be removed before our democratic health can be realized. Segregation is wrong because it is nothing but a new form of slavery covered up with certain niceties of complexity. Segregation is wrong because it is a system of adultery perpetuated by an illicit intercourse between injustice and immorality. And in Birmingham, Alabama, and all over the South and all over the nation, we are simply saying that we will no longer sell our birthright of freedom for a mess of segregated pottage. In a real sense, we are through with segregation now, henceforth, and forevermore.

Now Birmingham and the freedom struggle tell us something else. They reveal to us that the Negro has a new sense of dignity and a new sense of self-respect. For years, I think we all will agree that probably the most damaging effect of segregation has been what it has done to the soul of the segregated as well as the segregator. It has given the segregator a false sense of superiority and it has left the segregated with a false sense of inferiority. And so because of the legacy of slavery and segregation, many Negroes lost faith in themselves and many felt that they were inferior.

But then something happened to the Negro. Circumstances made it possible and necessary for him to travel more: the coming of the automobile, the upheavals of two world wars, the Great Depression. And so his rural, plantation background gradually gave way to urban, industrial life. And even his economic life was rising through the growth of industry, the influence of organized labor, expanded educational opportunities. And even his cultural life was rising through the steady decline of crippling illiteracy. And all of these forces conjoined to cause the Negro to take a new look at himself. Negro masses [*Applause*], Negro masses all over began to re-evaluate themselves, and the Negro came to feel that he was somebody. His religion revealed to him [*Applause*], his religion revealed to him that God loves all of his children, and that all men are made in His image, and that figuratively speaking, every man from a bass-black to a treble-white is significant on God's keyboard.

So, the Negro can now unconsciously cry out with the eloquent poet,

Fleecy locks and black complexion
Cannot forfeit nature's claim.
Skin may differ, but affection

Dwells in black and white the same.
Were I so tall as to reach the pole
Or to grasp at the ocean at a span,
I must be measured by my soul
The mind is the standard of the man.

But these events that are taking place in our nation tell us something else. They tell us that the Negro and his allies in the white community now recognize the urgency of the moment. I know we have heard a lot of cries saying, "Slow up and cool off." We still hear these cries. They are telling us over and over again that you're pushing things too fast, and so they're saying, "Cool off." Well, the only answer that we can give to that is that we've cooled off all too long, and that is the danger. There's always the danger if you cool off too much that you will end up in a deep freeze. "Well," they're saying, "you need to put on brakes." The only answer that we can give to that is that the motor's now cranked up and we're moving up the highway of freedom toward the city of equality, and we can't afford to stop now because our nation has a date with destiny. We must keep moving.

Then there is another cry. They say, "Why don't you do it in a gradual manner?" Well, gradualism is little more than escapism and do-nothingism, which ends up in stand-stillism. We know that our brothers and sisters in Africa and Asia are moving with jet-like speed toward the goal of political independence. And in some communities we are still moving at horse-and-buggy pace toward the gaining of a hamburger and a cup of coffee at a lunch counter.

And so we must say, now is the time to make real the promises of democracy. Now is the time to transform this pending national elegy into a creative psalm of brotherhood. Now is the time to lift our nation. Now is the time to lift our nation from the quicksands of racial injustice to the solid rock of racial justice. Now is the time to get rid of segregation and discrimination. Now is the time.

And so this social revolution taking place can be summarized in

three little words. They are not big words. One does not need an extensive vocabulary to understand them. They are the words "all," "here,"
and "now." We want *all* of our rights, we want them *here*, and we want
them *now*.

[*Recording interrupted*]

Now the other thing that we must see about this struggle is that by
and large it has been a nonviolent struggle. Let nobody make you feel
that those who are engaged or who are engaging in the demonstrations
in communities all across the South are resorting to violence; these are
few in number. For we've come to see the power of nonviolence. We've
come to see that this method is not a weak method, for it's the strong
man who can stand up amid opposition, who can stand up amid violence being inflicted upon him and not retaliate with violence.

You see, this method has a way of disarming the opponent. It exposes
his moral defenses. It weakens his morale, and at the same time it works
on his conscience, and he just doesn't know what to do. If he doesn't beat
you, wonderful. If he beats you, you develop the quiet courage of accept-
ing blows without retaliating. If he doesn't put you in jail, wonderful.
Nobody with any sense likes to go to jail. But if he puts you in jail, you go
in that jail and transform it from a dungeon of shame to a haven of freedom and human dignity. And even if he tries to kill you, you'll develop
the inner conviction that there are some things so dear, some things so
precious, some things so eternally true, that they are worth dying for.
And I submit to you that if a man has not discovered something that he
will die for, he isn't fit to live.

This method has wrought wonders. As a result of the nonviolent Freedom Ride movement, segregation in public transportation has almost
passed away absolutely in the South. As a result of the sit-in movement
at lunch counters, more than 285 cities have now integrated their lunch
counters in the South. I say to you, there is power in this method.

And I think by following this approach it will also help us to go into
the new age that is emerging with the right attitude. For nonviolence
not only calls upon its adherents to avoid external physical violence, but

it calls upon them to avoid internal violence of spirit. It calls on them to engage in that something called love. And I know it is difficult sometimes. When I say "love" at this point, I'm not talking about an affectionate emotion. It's nonsense to urge people, oppressed people, to love their oppressors in an affectionate sense. I'm talking about something much deeper. I'm talking about a sort of understanding, creative, redemptive goodwill for all men.

We are coming to see now, the psychiatrists are saying to us, that many of the strange things that happen in the subconscience, many of the inner conflicts, are rooted in hate. And so they are saying, "Love or perish." But Jesus told us this a long time ago. And I can still hear that voice crying through the vista of time, saying, "Love your enemies, bless them that curse you, pray for them that despitefully use you." And there is still a voice saying to every potential Peter, "Put up your sword." History is replete with the bleached bones of nations, history is cluttered with the wreckage of communities that failed to follow this command. And isn't it marvelous to have a method of struggle where it is possible to stand up against an unjust system, fight it with all of your might, never accept it, and yet not stoop to violence and hatred in the process? This is what we have.

Now there is a magnificent new militancy within the Negro community all across this nation. And I welcome this as a marvelous development. The Negro of America is saying he's determined to be free and he is militant enough to stand up. But this new militancy must not lead us to the position of distrusting every white person who lives in the United States. There are some white people in this country who are as determined to see the Negro free as we are to be free. This new militancy must be kept within understanding boundaries.

And then another thing I can understand. We've been pushed around so long; we've been the victims of lynching mobs so long; we've been the victims of economic injustice so long—still the last hired and the first fired all over this nation. And I know the temptation. I can understand from a psychological point of view why some caught up in the clutches of the injustices surrounding them almost respond with bitterness and come to the conclusion that the problem can't be solved within, and they talk about getting away from it in terms of racial separation. But even though I can understand it psychologically, I must say to you this afternoon that this isn't the way. Black supremacy is as dangerous as white supremacy. No, I hope you will allow me to say to you this afternoon that God is not interested merely in the freedom of black men and brown men and yellow men. God is interested in the freedom of the whole human race. And I believe that with this philosophy and this determined struggle we will be able to go on in the days ahead and transform the jangling discords of our nation into a beautiful symphony of brotherhood.

As I move toward my conclusion, you're asking, I'm sure, "What can we do here in Detroit to help in the struggle in the South?" Well, there are several things that you can do. One of them you've done already, and I hope you will do it in even greater dimensions before we leave this meeting. [*Recording interrupted*]

Now the second thing that you can do to help us down in Alabama and Mississippi and all over the South is to work with determination to get rid of any segregation and discrimination in Detroit, realizing that injustice anywhere is a threat to justice everywhere. And we've got to come to see that the problem of racial injustice is a national problem. No community in this country can boast of clean hands in the area of brotherhood. Now in the North it's different in that it doesn't have the legal sanction that it has in the South. But it has its subtle and hidden forms and it exists in three areas: in the area of employment discrimination, in the area of housing discrimination, and in the area of *de facto* segregation in the public schools. And we must come to see that *de facto* segregation in the North is just as injurious as the actual segregation in the South. And so if you want to help us in Alabama and Mississippi and over the South, do all that you can to get rid of the problem here.

And then we also need your support in order to get the civil rights bill that the President is offering passed. And there's a reality, let's not fool ourselves: this bill isn't going to get through if we don't put some work in it and some determined pressure. And this is why I've said that in order to get this bill through, we've got to arouse the conscience of the nation, and we ought to march to Washington more than 100,000 in order to say [*Applause*], in order to say that we are determined, and in order to engage in a nonviolent protest to keep this issue before the conscience of the nation.

And if we will do this we will be able to bring that new day of freedom into being. If we will do this we will be able to make the American dream a reality. And I do not want to give you the impression that it's going to be easy. There can be no great social gain without individual pain. And before the victory for brotherhood is won, some will have to get scarred up a bit. Before the victory is won, some more will be thrown into jail. Before the victory is won, some, like Medgar Evers, may have to face physical death. But if physical death is the price that some must pay to free their children and their white brothers from an eternal psychological death, then nothing can be more redemptive. Before the victory is won, some will be misunderstood and called bad names, but we must go on with a determination and with a faith that this problem can be solved.

And so I go back to the South not in despair. I go back to the South not with a feeling that we are caught in a dark dungeon that will never lead to a way out. I go back believing that the new day is coming. And so this afternoon, I have a dream. It is a dream deeply rooted in the American dream.

I have a dream that one day, right down in Georgia and Mississippi and Alabama, the sons of former slaves and the sons of former slave owners will be able to live together as brothers.

I have a dream this afternoon that one day [*Applause*], one day little white children and little Negro children will be able to join hands as brothers and sisters.

I have a dream this afternoon that one day [*Applause*], that one day men will no longer burn down houses and the church of God simply because people want to be free.

I have a dream this afternoon that there will be a day that we will no longer face the atrocities that Emmett Till had to face or Medgar Evers had to face, that all men can live with dignity.

I have a dream this afternoon that my four little children [*Applause*], that my four little children will not come up in the same young days that I came up within, but they will be judged on the basis of the content of their character, not the color of their skin.

I have a dream this afternoon that one day right here in Detroit, Negroes will be able to buy a house or rent a house anywhere that their money will carry them and they will be able to get a job.

Yes, I have a dream this afternoon that one day in this land the words of Amos will become real and "justice will roll down like waters, and righteousness like a mighty stream."

I have a dream this evening that one day we will recognize the words of Jefferson that "all men are created equal, that they are endowed by their Creator with certain unalienable Rights, that among these are Life, Liberty and the pursuit of Happiness." I have a dream this afternoon.

I have a dream that one day "every valley shall be exalted, and every hill and mountain shall be made low; the rough places would be made plain; and the crooked places will be made straight; and the glory of the Lord shall be revealed, and all flesh shall see it together."

I have a dream this afternoon that the brotherhood of man will become a reality in this day.

And with this faith I will go out and carve a tunnel of hope through the mountain of despair. With this faith, I will go out with you and transform dark yesterdays into bright tomorrows. With this faith, we will be able to achieve this new day when all of God's children, black men and white men, Jews and Gentiles, Protestants and Catholics, will be able to join hands and sing with the Negroes in the spiritual of old:

Free at last! Free at last!
Thank God almighty, we are free at last!

Reflection Questions

1. Why do the words "all," "here," and "now" make such a rallying cry? How does Dr. King use them to encourage the crowd?

2. Again, Dr. King draws on nonviolence as the most effective method for providing equal rights to African Americans. What remains consistent about his message? Has anything changed? What is the significance of the consistency? The change?

3. What warnings does Dr. King give regarding the "new militancy" among some African Americans?

4. Dr. King talks about de facto segregation in the North. What is de facto segregation? Describe one form of de facto segregation that exists in your community or elsewhere in the United States today.

Letter from Birmingham Jail

On April 12, 1963, Dr. King and some of his followers were arrested in Birmingham, Alabama, for violating a city order against public protest, and Dr. King was placed in solitary confinement. Here, in one of his most famous pieces of writing, Dr. King defends non-violent resistance as necessary to "help men rise from the depths of prejudice and racism to the majestic heights of understanding and brotherhood." Dr. King challenges white moderates who claim to be sympathetic to the cause but fail to take action to stop injustice. Though the letter was never sent to the eight ministers it was intended for, it was published and distributed in a variety of formats, such as newspapers, magazines, and pamphlets, before King revised it a year later and included it in his memoir of the Birmingham campaign, *Why We Can't Wait*.

As originally written by Dr. King:

AUTHOR'S NOTE: This response to a published statement by eight fellow clergymen from Alabama (Bishop C. C. J. Carpenter, Bishop Joseph A. Durick, Rabbi Hilton L. Grafman, Bishop Paul Hardin, Bishop Holan B. Harmon, the Reverend George M. Murray, the Reverend Edward V. Ramage and the Reverend Earl Stallings) was composed under somewhat constricting circumstances. Begun on the margins of the newspaper in which the statement appeared while I was in jail, the letter was continued on scraps of writing paper supplied by a friendly Negro trusty, and concluded on a pad my attorneys were eventually permitted to leave me. Although the text remains in substance unaltered, I have indulged in the author's prerogative of polishing it for publication.

From Why We Can't Wait *(Harper & Row, 1963, 1964, reprinted by Beacon Press, 2010).*

April 16, 1963

MY DEAR FELLOW CLERGYMEN:

While confined here in the Birmingham city jail, I came across your recent statement calling my present activities "unwise and untimely." Seldom do I pause to answer criticism of my work and ideas. If I sought to answer all the criticisms that cross my desk, my secretaries would have little time for anything other than such correspondence in the course of the day, and I would have no time for constructive work. But since I feel that you are men of genuine good will and that your criticisms are sincerely set forth, I want to try to answer your statement in what I hope will be patient and reasonable terms.

I think I should indicate why I am here in Birmingham, since you have been influenced by the view which argues against "outsiders coming in." I have the honor of serving as president of the Southern Christian Leadership Conference, an organization operating in every southern state, with headquarters in Atlanta, Georgia. We have some eighty-five affiliated organizations across the South, and one of them is the Alabama Christian Movement for Human Rights. Frequently we share staff, educational and financial resources with our affiliates. Several months ago the affiliate here in Birmingham asked us to be on call to engage in a nonviolent direct-action program if such were deemed necessary. We readily consented, and when the hour came we lived up to our promise. So I, along with several members of my staff, am here because I was invited here. I am here because I have organizational ties here.

But more basically, I am in Birmingham because injustice is here. Just as the prophets of the eighth century B.C. left their villages and carried their "thus saith the Lord" far beyond the boundaries of their home towns, and just as the Apostle Paul left his village of Tarsus and carried the gospel of Jesus Christ to the far corners of the Greco-Roman world, so am I compelled to carry the gospel of freedom beyond my own home town. Like Paul, I must constantly respond to the Macedonian call for aid.

Moreover, I am cognizant of the interrelatedness of all communities and states. I cannot sit idly by in Atlanta and not be concerned about what happens in Birmingham. Injustice anywhere is a threat to justice everywhere. We are caught in an inescapable network of mutuality, tied in a single garment of destiny. Whatever affects one directly, affects all indirectly. Never again can we afford to live with the narrow, provincial "outside agitator" idea. Anyone who lives inside the United States can never be considered an outsider anywhere within its bounds.

You deplore the demonstrations taking place in Birmingham. But your statement, I am sorry to say, fails to express a similar concern for the conditions that brought about the demonstrations. I am sure that none of you would want to rest content with the superficial kind of social analysis that deals merely with effects and does not grapple with underlying causes. It is unfortunate that demonstrations are taking place in Birmingham, but it is even more unfortunate that the city's white power structure left the Negro community with no alternative.

In any nonviolent campaign there are four basic steps: collection of the facts to determine whether injustices exist; negotiation; self-purification; and direct action. We have gone through all these steps in Birmingham. There can be no gainsaying the fact that racial injustice engulfs this community. Birmingham is probably the most thoroughly segregated city in the United States. Its ugly record of brutality is widely known. Negroes have experienced grossly unjust treatment in the courts. There have been more unsolved bombings of Negro homes and churches in Birmingham than in any other city in the nation. These are the hard, brutal facts of the case. On the basis of these conditions, Negro leaders sought to negotiate with the city fathers. But the latter consistently refused to engage in good-faith negotiation.

Then, last September, came the opportunity to talk with leaders of Birmingham's economic community. In the course of the negotiations, certain promises were made by the merchants—for example, to remove the stores' humiliating racial signs. On the basis of these promises, the Reverend Fred Shuttlesworth and the leaders of the Alabama Christian

Movement for Human Rights agreed to a moratorium on all demonstrations. As the weeks and months went by, we realized that we were the victims of a broken promise. A few signs, briefly removed, returned; the others remained.

As in so many past experiences, our hopes had been blasted, and the shadow of deep disappointment settled upon us. We had no alternative except to prepare for direct action, whereby we would present our very bodies as a means of laying our case before the conscience of the local and the national community. Mindful of the difficulties involved, we decided to undertake a process of self-purification. We began a series of workshops on nonviolence, and we repeatedly asked ourselves: "Are you able to accept blows without retaliating?" "Are you able to endure the ordeal of jail?" We decided to schedule our direct-action program for the Easter season, realizing that except for Christmas, this is the main shopping period of the year. Knowing that a strong economic-withdrawal program would be the by-product of direct action, we felt that this would be the best time to bring pressure to bear on the merchants for the needed change.

Then it occurred to us that Birmingham's mayoralty election was coming up in March, and we speedily decided to postpone action until after election day. When we discovered that the Commissioner of Public Safety, Eugene "Bull" Connor, had piled up enough votes to be in the run-off, we decided again to postpone action until the day after the run-off so that the demonstrations could not be used to cloud the issues. Like many others, we waited to see Mr. Connor defeated, and to this end we endured postponement after postponement. Having aided in this community need, we felt that our direct-action program could be delayed no longer.

You may well ask: "Why direct action? Why sit-ins, marches and so forth? Isn't negotiation a better path?" You are quite right in calling for negotiation. Indeed, this is the very purpose of direct action. Nonviolent direct action seeks to create such a crisis and foster such a tension that a community which has constantly refused to negotiate is forced to confront the issue. It seeks so to dramatize the issue that it can no longer be ignored. My citing the creation of tension as part of the work of the nonviolent-resister may sound rather shocking. But I must confess that I am not afraid of the word "tension." I have earnestly opposed violent tension, but there is a type of constructive, nonviolent tension which is necessary for growth. Just as Socrates felt that it was necessary to create a tension in the mind so that individuals could rise from the bondage of myths and half-truths to the unfettered realm of creative analysis and objective appraisal, so must we see the need for nonviolent gadflies to create the kind of tension in society that will help men rise from the dark depths of prejudice and racism to the majestic heights of understanding and brotherhood.

The purpose of our direct-action program is to create a situation so crisis-packed that it will inevitably open the door to negotiation. I therefore concur with you in your call for negotiation. Too long has our beloved Southland been bogged down in a tragic effort to live in monologue rather than dialogue.

One of the basic points in your statement is that the action that I and my associates have taken in Birmingham is untimely. Some have asked: "Why didn't you give the new city administration time to act?" The only answer that I can give to this query is that the new Birmingham administration must be prodded about as much as the outgoing one, before it will act. We are sadly mistaken if we feel that the election of Albert Boutwell as mayor will bring the millennium to Birmingham. While Mr. Boutwell is a much more gentle person than Mr. Connor, they are both segregationists, dedicated to maintenance of the status quo. I have hope that Mr. Boutwell will be reasonable enough to see the futility of massive resistance to desegregation. But he will not see this without pressure from devotees of civil rights. My friends, I must say to you that we have not made a single gain in civil rights without determined legal and nonviolent pressure. Lamentably, it is an historical fact that privileged groups seldom give up their privileges voluntarily. Individuals may see the moral light and voluntarily give up their unjust posture; but, as Reinhold Niebuhr has reminded us, groups tend to be more immoral than individuals.

We know through painful experience that freedom is never voluntarily given by the oppressor; it must be demanded by the oppressed. Frankly, I have yet to engage in a direct-action campaign that was "well timed" in the view of those who have not suffered unduly from the disease of segregation. For years now I have heard the word "Wait!" It rings in the ear of every Negro with piercing familiarity. This "Wait" has almost always meant "Never." We must come to see, with one of our distinguished jurists, that "justice too long delayed is justice denied."

We have waited for more than 340 years for our constitutional and God-given rights. The nations of Asia and Africa are moving with jet-like speed toward gaining political independence, but we still creep at horse-and-buggy pace toward gaining a cup of coffee at a lunch counter. Perhaps it is easy for those who have never felt the stinging darts of segregation to say, "Wait." But when you have seen vicious mobs lynch your mothers and fathers at will and drown your sisters and brothers at whim; when you have seen hate-filled policemen curse, kick and even kill your black brothers and sisters; when you see the vast majority of your twenty million Negro brothers smothering in an airtight cage of poverty in the midst of an affluent society; when you suddenly find your tongue twisted and your speech stammering as you seek to explain to your six-year-old daughter why she can't go to the public amusement park that has just been advertised on television, and see tears welling up in her eyes when she is told that Funtown is closed to colored children, and see ominous clouds of inferiority beginning to form in her little mental sky, and see her beginning to distort her personality by developing an unconscious bitterness toward white people; when you have to concoct an answer for a five-year-old son who is asking: "Daddy, why do white people treat colored people so mean?"; when you take a cross-country drive and find it necessary to sleep night after night in the uncomfortable corners of your automobile because no motel will accept you; when you are humiliated day in and day out by nagging signs reading "white" and "colored"; when your first name becomes "nigger," your middle name becomes "boy" (however old you are) and your last name becomes "John," and your wife and mother are never given the respected title "Mrs."; when you are harried by day and haunted by night by the fact that you are a Negro, living constantly at tiptoe stance, never quite knowing what to expect next, and are plagued with inner fears and outer resentments; when you are forever fighting a degenerating sense of "nobodiness"—then you will understand why we find it difficult to wait. There comes a time when the cup of endurance runs over, and men are no longer willing to be plunged into the abyss of despair. I hope, sirs, you can understand our legitimate and unavoidable impatience.

You express a great deal of anxiety over our willingness to break laws. This is certainly a legitimate concern. Since we so diligently urge people to obey the Supreme Court's decision of 1954 outlawing segregation in the public schools, at first glance it may seem rather paradoxical for us consciously to break laws. One may well ask: "How can you advocate breaking some laws and obeying others?" The answer lies in the fact that there are two types of laws: just and unjust. I would be the first to advocate obeying just laws. One has not only a legal but a moral responsibility to obey just laws. Conversely, one has a moral responsibility to disobey unjust laws. I would agree with St. Augustine that "an unjust law is no law at all."

Now, what is the difference between the two? How does one determine whether a law is just or unjust? A just law is a man-made code that squares with the moral law or the law of God. An unjust law is a code that is out of harmony with the moral law. To put it in the terms of St. Thomas Aquinas: An unjust law is a human law that is not rooted in eternal law and natural law. Any law that uplifts human personality is just. Any law that degrades human personality is unjust. All segregation statutes are unjust because segregation distorts the soul and damages the personality. It gives the segregator a false sense of superiority and the segregated a false sense of inferiority. Segregation, to use the terminology of the Jewish philosopher Martin Buber, substitutes an "I-it" relationship for an "I-thou" relationship and ends up relegating persons to the status of things. Hence segregation is not only politically, economically and sociologically unsound, it is morally wrong and sinful. Paul Tillich has said that sin is separation. Is not segregation an existential expression of man's tragic separation, his awful estrangement, his terrible sinfulness? Thus it is that I can urge men to obey the 1954 decision of the Supreme Court, for it is morally right; and I can urge them to disobey segregation ordinances, for they are morally wrong.

Let us consider a more concrete example of just and unjust laws. An unjust law is a code that a numerical or power majority group compels a minority group to obey but does not make binding on itself. This is *difference* made legal. By the same token, a just law is a code that a majority compels a minority to follow and that it is willing to follow itself. This is *sameness* made legal.

Let me give another explanation. A law is unjust if it is inflicted on a minority that, as a result of being denied the right to vote, had no part in enacting or devising the law. Who can say that the legislature of Alabama which set up that state's segregation laws was democratically elected? Throughout Alabama all sorts of devious methods are used to prevent Negroes from becoming registered voters, and there are some counties in which, even though Negroes constitute a majority of the population, not a single Negro is registered. Can any law enacted under such circumstances be considered democratically structured?

Sometimes a law is just on its face and unjust in its application. For instance, I have been arrested on a charge of parading without a permit. Now, there is nothing wrong in having an ordinance which requires a permit for a parade. But such an ordinance becomes unjust when it is used to maintain segregation and to deny citizens the First-Amendment privilege of peaceful assembly and protest.

I hope you are able to see the distinction I am trying to point out. In no sense do I advocate evading or defying the law, as would the rabid segregationist. That would lead to anarchy. One who breaks an unjust law must do so openly, lovingly, and with a willingness to accept the penalty. I submit that an individual who breaks a law that conscience tells him is unjust, and who willingly accepts the penalty of imprisonment in order to arouse the conscience of the community over its injustice, is in reality expressing the highest respect for law.

Of course, there is nothing new about this kind of civil disobedience. It was evidenced sublimely in the refusal of Shadrach, Meshach and Abednego to obey the laws of Nebuchadnezzar, on the ground that a higher moral law was at stake. It was practiced superbly by the early Christians, who were willing to face hungry lions and the excruciating pain of chopping blocks rather than submit to certain unjust laws of the Roman Empire. To a degree, academic freedom is a reality today because Socrates practiced civil disobedience. In our own nation, the Boston Tea Party represented a massive act of civil disobedience.

We should never forget that everything Adolf Hitler did in Germany was "legal" and everything the Hungarian freedom fighters did in Hungary was "illegal." It was "illegal" to aid and comfort a Jew in Hitler's Germany. Even so, I am sure that, had I lived in Germany at the time, I would have aided and comforted my Jewish brothers. If today I lived in a Communist country where certain principles dear to the Christian faith are suppressed, I would openly advocate disobeying that country's antireligious laws.

I must make two honest confessions to you, my Christian and Jewish brothers. First, I must confess that over the past few years I have been gravely disappointed with the white moderate. I have almost reached the regrettable conclusion that the Negro's great stumbling block in his stride toward freedom is not the White Citizens' Counciler or the Ku Klux Klanner, but the white moderate, who is more devoted to "order" than to justice; who prefers a negative peace which is the absence of tension to a positive peace which is the presence of justice; who constantly says: "I agree with you in the goal you seek, but I cannot agree with your methods of direct action"; who paternalistically believes he can set the timetable for another man's freedom; who lives by a mythical concept of time and who constantly advises the Negro to wait for a "more convenient season." Shallow understanding from people of good will is more frustrating than absolute misunderstanding from people of ill will. Lukewarm acceptance is much more bewildering than outright rejection.

I had hoped that the white moderate would understand that law and order exist for the purpose of establishing justice and that when they fail in this purpose they become the dangerously structured dams that block the flow of social progress. I had hoped that the white moderate would understand that the present tension in the South is a necessary phase of the transition from an obnoxious negative peace, in which the Negro passively accepted his unjust plight, to a substantive and positive peace, in which all men will respect the dignity and worth of human personality. Actually, we who engage in nonviolent direct action are not the creators of tension. We merely bring to the surface the hidden tension that is already alive. We bring it out in the open, where it can be seen and dealt with. Like a boil that can never be cured so long as it is covered up but must be opened with all its ugliness to the natural medicines of air and light, injustice must be exposed, with all the tension its exposure creates, to the light of human conscience and the air of national opinion before it can be cured.

In your statement you assert that our actions, even though peaceful, must be condemned because they precipitate violence. But is this a logical assertion? Isn't this like condemning a robbed man because his possession of money precipitated the evil act of robbery? Isn't this like condemning Socrates because his unswerving commitment to truth and his philosophical inquiries precipitated the act by the misguided populace in which they made him drink hemlock? Isn't this like condemning Jesus because his unique God-consciousness and never-ceasing devotion to God's will precipitated the evil act of crucifixion? We must come to see that, as the federal courts have consistently affirmed, it is wrong to urge an individual to cease his efforts to gain his basic constitutional rights because the quest may precipitate violence. Society must protect the robbed and punish the robber.

I had also hoped that the white moderate would reject the myth concerning time in relation to the struggle for freedom. I have just received a letter from a white brother in Texas. He writes: "All Christians know that the colored people will receive equal rights eventually, but it is possible that you are in too great a religious hurry. It has taken Christianity almost two thousand years to accomplish what it has. The teachings of Christ take time to come to earth." Such an attitude stems from a tragic misconception of time, from the strangely irrational notion that there is something in the very flow of time that will inevitably cure all ills. Actually, time itself is neutral; it can be used either destructively or constructively. More and more I feel that the people of ill will have used time much more effectively than have the people of good will. We will have to repent in this generation not merely for the hateful words and actions of the bad people but for the appalling silence of the good people. Human progress never rolls in on wheels of inevitability; it comes through the tireless efforts of men willing to be coworkers with God, and without this hard work, time itself becomes an ally of the forces of social stagnation. We must use time creatively, in the knowledge that the time is always ripe to do right. Now is the time to make real the promise of democracy and transform our pending national elegy into a creative psalm of brotherhood. Now is the time to lift our national policy from the quicksand of racial injustice to the solid rock of human dignity.

You speak of our activity in Birmingham as extreme. At first I was rather disappointed that fellow clergymen would see my nonviolent efforts as those of an extremist. I began thinking about the fact that I stand in the middle of two opposing forces in the Negro community. One is a force of complacency, made up in part of Negroes who, as a result of long years of oppression, are so drained of self-respect and a sense of "somebodiness" that they have adjusted to segregation; and in part of a few middle-class Negroes who, because of a degree of academic and economic security and because in some ways they profit by segregation, have become insensitive to the problems of the masses. The other force is one of bitterness and hatred, and it comes perilously close to advocating violence. It is expressed in the various black nationalist groups that are springing up across the nation, the largest and best known being Elijah Muhammad's Muslim movement. Nourished by the Negro's frustration over the continued existence of racial discrimination, this movement is made up of people who have lost faith in America, who have absolutely repudiated Christianity, and who have concluded that the white man is an incorrigible "devil."

I have tried to stand between these two forces, saying that we need emulate neither the "do-nothingism" of the complacent nor the hatred and despair of the black nationalist. For there is the more excellent way of love and nonviolent protest. I am grateful to God that, through the influence of the Negro church, the way of nonviolence became an integral part of our struggle.

If this philosophy had not emerged, by now many streets of the South would, I am convinced, be flowing with blood. And I am further convinced that if our white brothers dismiss as "rabble-rousers" and "outside agitators" those of us who employ nonviolent direct action, and if they refuse to support our nonviolent efforts, millions of Negroes will, out of frustration and despair, seek solace and security in black-nationalist ideologies—a development that would inevitably lead to a frightening racial nightmare.

Oppressed people cannot remain oppressed forever. The yearning for freedom eventually manifests itself, and that is what has happened to the American Negro. Something within has reminded him of his birthright of freedom, and something without has reminded him that it can be gained. Consciously or unconsciously, he has been caught up by the *Zeitgeist*, and with his black brothers of Africa and his brown and yellow brothers of Asia, South America and the Caribbean, the United States Negro is moving with a sense of great urgency toward the promised land of racial justice. If one recognizes this vital urge that has engulfed the Negro community, one should readily understand why public demonstrations are taking place. The Negro has many pent-up resentments and latent frustrations, and he must release them. So let him march; let him make prayer pilgrimages to the city hall; let him go on freedom rides— and try to understand why he must do so. If his repressed emotions are not released in nonviolent ways, they will seek expression through violence; this is not a threat but a fact of history. So I have not said to my people: "Get rid of your discontent." Rather, I have tried to say that this normal and healthy discontent can be channeled into the creative outlet of nonviolent direct action. And now this approach is being termed extremist.

But though I was initially disappointed at being categorized as an extremist, as I continued to think about the matter I gradually gained a measure of satisfaction from the label. Was not Jesus an extremist for love: "Love your enemies, bless them that curse you, do good to them that hate you, and pray for them which despitefully use you, and persecute you." Was not Amos an extremist for justice: "Let justice roll down like waters and righteousness like an ever-flowing stream." Was not Paul an extremist for the Christian gospel: "I bear in my body the marks of the Lord Jesus." Was not Martin Luther an extremist: "Here I stand; I cannot do otherwise, so help me God." And John Bunyan: "I will stay in jail to the end of my days before I make a butchery of my conscience." And Abraham Lincoln: "This nation cannot survive half slave and half free." And Thomas Jefferson: "We hold these truths to be self-evident, that all men are created equal ..." So the question is not whether we will be extremists, but what kind of extremists we will be. Will we be extremists for hate or for love? Will we be extremists for the preservation of injustice or for the extension of justice? In that dramatic scene on Calvary's hill three men were crucified. We must never forget that all three were crucified for the same crime—the crime of extremism. Two were extremists for immorality, and thus fell below their environment. The other, Jesus Christ, was an extremist for love, truth and goodness, and thereby rose above his environment. Perhaps the South, the nation and the world are in dire need of creative extremists.

I had hoped that the white moderate would see this need. Perhaps I was too optimistic; perhaps I expected too much. I suppose I should have realized that few members of the oppressor race can understand the deep groans and passionate yearnings of the oppressed race, and still fewer have the vision to see that injustice must be rooted out by strong, persistent and determined action. I am thankful, however, that some of our white brothers in the South have grasped the meaning of this social revolution and committed themselves to it. They are still all too few in quantity, but they are big in quality. Some—such as Ralph McGill, Lillian Smith, Harry Golden, James McBride Dabbs, Ann Braden and Sarah Patton Boyle—have written about our struggle in eloquent and prophetic terms. Others have marched with us down nameless streets of the South. They have languished in filthy, roach-infested jails, suffering the abuse and brutality of policemen who view them as "dirty nigger-lovers." Unlike so many of their moderate brothers and sisters, they have recognized the urgency of the moment and sensed the need for powerful "action" antidotes to combat the disease of segregation.

Let me take note of my other major disappointment. I have been so greatly disappointed with the white church and its leadership. Of course, there are some notable exceptions. I am not unmindful of the fact that each of you has taken some significant stands on this issue. I commend you, Reverend Stallings, for your Christian stand on this past Sunday, in welcoming Negroes to your worship service on a nonsegregated basis. I commend the Catholic leaders of this state for integrating Spring Hill College several years ago.

But despite these notable exceptions, I must honestly reiterate that I have been disappointed with the church. I do not say this as one of those negative critics who can always find something wrong with the church. I say this as a minister of the gospel, who loves the church; who was nurtured in its bosom; who has been sustained by its spiritual blessings and who will remain true to it as long as the cord of life shall lengthen.

When I was suddenly catapulted into the leadership of the bus protest in Montgomery, Alabama, a few years ago, I felt we would be supported by the white church. I felt that the white ministers, priests and rabbis of the South would be among our strongest allies. Instead, some have been outright opponents, refusing to understand the freedom movement and misrepresenting its leaders; all too many others have been more cautious than courageous and have remained silent behind the anesthetizing security of stained-glass windows.

In spite of my shattered dreams, I came to Birmingham with the hope that the white religious leadership of this community would see the justice of our cause and, with deep moral concern, would serve as the channel through which our just grievances could reach the power structure. I had hoped that each of you would understand. But again I have been disappointed.

I have heard numerous southern religious leaders admonish their worshipers to comply with a desegregation decision because it is the law, but I have longed to hear white ministers declare: "Follow this decree because integration is morally right and because the Negro is your brother." In the midst of blatant injustices inflicted upon the Negro, I have watched white churchmen stand on the sideline and mouth pious irrelevancies and sanctimonious trivialities. In the midst of a mighty struggle to rid our nation of racial and economic injustice, I have heard many ministers say: "Those are social issues, with which the gospel has no real concern." And I have watched many churches commit themselves to a completely otherworldly religion which makes a strange, un-Biblical distinction between body and soul, between the sacred and the secular.

I have traveled the length and breadth of Alabama, Mississippi and all the other southern states. On sweltering summer days and crisp autumn mornings I have looked at the South's beautiful churches with their lofty spires pointing heavenward. I have beheld the impressive outlines of her massive religious-education buildings. Over and over I have found myself asking: "What kind of people worship here? Who is their God? Where were their voices when the lips of Governor Barnett dripped with words of interposition and nullification? Where were they when Governor Wallace gave a clarion call for defiance and hatred? Where were their voices of support when bruised and weary Negro men and women decided to rise from the dark dungeons of complacency to the bright hills of creative protest?"

Yes, these questions are still in my mind. In deep disappointment I have wept over the laxity of the church. But be assured that my tears have been tears of love. There can be no deep disappointment where there is not deep love. Yes, I love the church. How could I do otherwise? I am in the rather unique position of being the son, the grandson and the great-grandson of preachers. Yes, I see the church as the body of Christ. But, oh! How we have blemished and scarred that body through social neglect and through fear of being non-conformists.

There was a time when the church was very powerful—in the time when the early Christians rejoiced at being deemed worthy to suffer for what they believed. In those days the church was not merely a thermometer that recorded the ideas and principles of popular opinion; it was a thermostat that transformed the mores of society. Whenever the early Christians entered a town, the people in power became disturbed and immediately sought to convict the Christians for being "disturbers of the peace" and "outside agitators." But the Christians pressed on, in the conviction that they were "a colony of heaven," called to obey God rather than man. Small in number, they were big in commitment. They were too God-intoxicated to be "astronomically intimidated." By their effort and example they brought an end to such ancient evils as infanticide and gladiatorial contests.

Things are different now. So often the contemporary church is a weak, ineffectual voice with an uncertain sound. So often it is an arch-defender of the status quo. Far from being disturbed by the presence of the church, the power structure of the average community is consoled by the church's silent—and often even vocal—sanction of things as they are.

But the judgment of God is upon the church as never before. If today's church does not recapture the sacrificial spirit of the early church, it will lose its authenticity, forfeit the loyalty of millions, and be dismissed as an irrelevant social club with no meaning for the twentieth century. Every day I meet young people whose disappointment with the church has turned into outright disgust.

Perhaps I have once again been too optimistic. Is organized religion too inextricably bound to the status quo to save our nation and the world? Perhaps I must turn my faith to the inner spiritual church, the church within the church, as the true *ekklesia* and the hope of the world. But again I am thankful to God that some noble souls from the ranks of organized religion have broken loose from the paralyzing chains of conformity and joined us as active partners in the struggle for freedom. They have left their secure congregations and walked the streets of Albany, Georgia, with us. They have gone down the highways of the South on tortuous rides for freedom. Yes, they have gone to jail with us. Some have been dismissed from their churches, have lost the support of their bishops and fellow ministers. But they have acted in the faith that right defeated is stronger than evil triumphant. Their witness has been the spiritual salt that has preserved the true meaning of the gospel in these troubled times. They have carved a tunnel of hope through the dark mountain of disappointment.

I hope the church as a whole will meet the challenge of this decisive hour. But even if the church does not come to the aid of justice, I have no despair about the future. I have no fear about the outcome of our struggle in Birmingham, even if our motives are at present misunderstood. We will reach the goal of freedom in Birmingham and all over the nation, because the goal of America is freedom. Abused and scorned though we may be, our destiny is tied up with America's destiny. Before the pilgrims landed at Plymouth, we were here. Before the pen of Jefferson etched the majestic words of the Declaration of Independence across the pages of history, we were here. For more than two centuries our forebears labored in this country without wages; they made cotton king; they built the homes of their masters while suffering gross injustice and shameful humiliation—and yet out of a bottomless vitality they continued to thrive and develop. If the inexpressible cruelties of slavery could not stop us, the opposition we now face will surely fail. We will win our freedom because the sacred heritage of our nation and the eternal will of God are embodied in our echoing demands.

Before closing I feel impelled to mention one other point in your statement that has troubled me profoundly. You warmly commended the Birmingham police force for keeping "order" and "preventing violence." I doubt that you would have so warmly commended the police force if you had seen its dogs sinking their teeth into unarmed, nonviolent Negroes. I doubt that you would so quickly commend the policemen if you were to observe their ugly and inhumane treatment of Negroes here in the city jail; if you were to watch them push and curse old Negro women and young Negro girls; if you were to see them slap and kick old Negro men and young boys; if you were to observe them, as they did on two occasions, refuse to give us food because we wanted to sing our grace together. I cannot join you in your praise of the Birmingham police department.

It is true that the police have exercised a degree of discipline in handling the demonstrators. In this sense they have conducted themselves rather "nonviolently" in public. But for what purpose? To preserve the evil system of segregation. Over the past few years I have consistently preached that nonviolence demands that the means we use must be as pure as the ends we seek. I have tried to make clear that it is wrong to use immoral means to attain moral ends. But now I must affirm that it is just as wrong, or perhaps even more so, to use moral means to preserve immoral ends. Perhaps Mr. Connor and his policemen have been rather nonviolent in public, as was Chief Pritchett in Albany, Georgia, but they have used the moral means of nonviolence to maintain the immoral end of racial injustice. As T. S. Eliot has said: "The last temptation is the greatest treason: To do the right deed for the wrong reason."

I wish you had commended the Negro sit-inners and demonstrators of Birmingham for their sublime courage, their willingness to suffer and their amazing discipline in the midst of great provocation. One day the South will recognize its real heroes. They will be the James Merediths, with the noble sense of purpose that enables them to face jeering and hostile mobs, and with the agonizing loneliness that characterizes the life of the pioneer. They will be old, oppressed, battered Negro women, symbolized in a seventy-two-year-old woman in Montgomery, Alabama, who rose up with a sense of dignity and with her people decided not to ride segregated buses, and who responded with ungrammatical profundity to one who inquired about her weariness: "My feets is tired, but my soul is at rest." They will be the young high school and college students, the young ministers of the gospel and a host of their elders, courageously and nonviolently sitting in at lunch counters and willingly going to jail for conscience's sake. One day the South will know that when these disinherited children of God sat down at lunch counters, they were in reality standing up for what is best in the American dream and for the most sacred values in our Judaeo-Christian heritage, thereby bringing our nation back to those great wells of democracy which were dug deep by the founding fathers in their formulation of the Constitution and the Declaration of Independence.

Never before have I written so long a letter. I'm afraid it is much too long to take your precious time. I can assure you that it would have been much shorter if I had been writing from a comfortable desk, but what else can one do when he is alone in a narrow jail cell, other than write long letters, think long thoughts and pray long prayers?

If I have said anything in this letter that overstates the truth and indicates an unreasonable impatience, I beg you to forgive me. If I have said anything that understates the truth and indicates my having a patience that allows me to settle for anything less than brotherhood, I beg God to forgive me.

I hope this letter finds you strong in the faith. I also hope that circumstances will soon make it possible for me to meet each of you, not as an integrationist or a civil-rights leader but as a fellow clergyman and a Christian brother. Let us all hope that the dark clouds of racial prejudice will soon pass away and the deep fog of misunderstanding will be lifted from our fear-drenched communities, and in some not too distant tomorrow the radiant stars of love and brotherhood will shine over our great nation with all their scintillating beauty.

> Yours for the cause of Peace and Brotherhood,
> MARTIN LUTHER KING, JR.

Reflection Questions

1. What rhetorical devices does Dr. King employ in this letter? What is the anticipated effect? Do you think he was successful?

2. Describe the calculations that Dr. King and other leaders employed leading up to direct action. What do these calculations suggest about Dr. King as a planner and about the movement in general?

3. What is the difference between a just and an unjust law? Are there laws that exist today that are just and unjust? How might you incorporate some of Dr. King's strategies to confront those unjust laws?

4. Dr. King is responding to accusations against him. How does he present his counterargument? What evidence does he use? How effective is his letter?

I Have a Dream

On August 28, 1963, over two hundred thousand demonstrators gathered on the Mall in Washington, DC, to conclude the March on Washington for Jobs and Freedom, where Dr. King delivered his best-known speech. Black labor leader A. Philip Randolph had called for the march in order to mobilize support for fair employment for blacks, civil rights legislation, and other reforms. At the end of a long program of speeches and freedom songs, Dr. King gave the short speech finished the previous night and then delivered extemporaneous remarks setting forth his "dream deeply rooted in the American dream." The speech drew on material and themes that Dr. King had brought forward in speeches and sermons before, including his speech in Detroit two months earlier. Following the march, Dr. King and other civil rights leaders met with President John Kennedy, who had introduced legislation that eventually became the Civil Rights Act of 1964.

I am happy to join with you today in what will go down in history as the greatest demonstration for freedom in the history of our nation.

Fivescore years ago, a great American, in whose symbolic shadow we stand today, signed the Emancipation Proclamation. This momentous decree came as a great beacon light of hope to millions of Negro

---

Delivered at the March on Washington for Jobs and Freedom, Washington, DC, August 28, 1963.

slaves who had been seared in the flames of withering injustice. It came as a joyous daybreak to end the long night of their captivity.

But one hundred years later, the Negro still is not free. One hundred years later, the life of the Negro is still sadly crippled by the manacles of segregation and the chains of discrimination. One hundred years later, the Negro lives on a lonely island of poverty in the midst of a vast ocean of material prosperity. One hundred years later, the Negro is still languished in the corners of American society and finds himself an exile in his own land. And so we've come here today to dramatize a shameful condition.

In a sense we've come to our nation's capital to cash a check. When the architects of our republic wrote the magnificent words of the Constitution and the Declaration of Independence, they were signing a promissory note to which every American was to fall heir. This note was a promise that all men, yes, black men as well as white men, would be guaranteed the "unalienable Rights of Life, Liberty, and the pursuit of Happiness." It is obvious today that America has defaulted on this promissory note insofar as her citizens of color are concerned. Instead of honoring this sacred obligation, America has given the Negro people a bad check, a check which has come back marked "insufficient funds."

But we refuse to believe that the bank of justice is bankrupt. We refuse to believe that there are insufficient funds in the great vaults of opportunity of this nation. And so we've come to cash this check, a check that will give us upon demand the riches of freedom and the security of justice.

We have also come to this hallowed spot to remind America of the fierce urgency of now. This is no time to engage in the luxury of cooling off or to take the tranquilizing drug of gradualism. Now is the time to make real the promises of democracy. Now is the time to rise from the dark and desolate valley of segregation to the sunlit path of racial justice. Now is the time to lift our nation from the quicksands of racial injustice to the solid rock of brotherhood. Now is the time to make justice a reality for all of God's children.

It would be fatal for the nation to overlook the urgency of the moment. This sweltering summer of the Negro's legitimate discontent will not pass until there is an invigorating autumn of freedom and equality. Nineteen sixty-three is not an end, but a beginning. And those who hope that the Negro needed to blow off steam and will now be content will have a rude awakening if the nation returns to business as usual. There will be neither rest nor tranquility in America until the Negro is granted his citizenship rights. The whirlwinds of revolt will continue to shake the foundations of our nation until the bright day of justice emerges.

But there is something that I must say to my people, who stand on the warm threshold which leads into the palace of justice: In the process of gaining our rightful place, we must not be guilty of wrongful deeds. Let us not seek to satisfy our thirst for freedom by drinking from the cup of bitterness and hatred. We must forever conduct our struggle on the high plane of dignity and discipline. We must not allow our creative protest to degenerate into physical violence. Again and again, we must rise to the majestic heights of meeting physical force with soul force. The marvelous new militancy which has engulfed the Negro community must not lead us to a distrust of all white people, for many of our white brothers, as evidenced by their presence here today, have come to realize that their destiny is tied up with our destiny. And they have come to realize that their freedom is inextricably bound to our freedom. We cannot walk alone.

And as we walk, we must make the pledge that we shall always march ahead. We cannot turn back. There are those who are asking the devotees of civil rights, "When will you be satisfied?"

We can never be satisfied as long as the Negro is the victim of the unspeakable horrors of police brutality. We can never be satisfied as long as our bodies, heavy with the fatigue of travel, cannot gain lodging in the motels of the highways and the hotels of the cities. We cannot be satisfied as long as the Negro's basic mobility is from a smaller ghetto to a larger one. We can never be satisfied as long as our children are stripped of their selfhood and robbed of their dignity by signs stating "for whites only." We cannot be satisfied as long as a Negro in Mississippi cannot vote and a Negro in New York believes he has nothing for which to vote. No, no, we are not satisfied, and we will not be satisfied until "justice rolls down like waters and righteousness like a mighty stream."

I am not unmindful that some of you have come here out of great trials and tribulations. Some of you have come fresh from narrow jail cells. Some of you have come from areas where your quest for freedom left you battered by the storms of persecution and staggered by the winds of police brutality. You have been the veterans of creative suffering. Continue to work with the faith that unearned suffering is redemptive. Go back to Mississippi, go back to Alabama, go back to South Carolina, go back to Georgia, go back to Louisiana, go back to the slums and ghettos of our northern cities, knowing that somehow this situation can and will be changed. Let us not wallow in the valley of despair.

I say to you today, my friends, so even though we face the difficulties of today and tomorrow, I still have a dream. It is a dream deeply rooted in the American dream.

I have a dream that one day this nation will rise up and live out the true meaning of its creed: "We hold these truths to be self-evident, that all men are created equal."

I have a dream that one day on the red hills of Georgia, the sons of former slaves and the sons of former slave owners will be able to sit down together at the table of brotherhood.

I have a dream that one day even the state of Mississippi, a state sweltering with the heat of injustice, sweltering with the heat of oppression, will be transformed into an oasis of freedom and justice.

I have a dream that my four little children will one day live in a nation where they will not be judged by the color of their skin but by the content of their character. I have a dream today.

I have a dream that one day down in Alabama, with its vicious racists, with its governor having his lips dripping with the words of "interposition" and "nullification," one day right there in Alabama little black boys and black girls will be able to join hands with little white boys and white girls as sisters and brothers. I have a dream today.

I have a dream that one day "every valley shall be exalted, and every hill and mountain shall be made low; the rough places will be made plain, and the crooked places will be made straight; and the glory of the Lord shall be revealed, and all flesh shall see it together."

This is our hope. This is the faith that I go back to the South with. With this faith we will be able to hew out of the mountain of despair a stone of hope. With this faith we will be able to transform the jangling discords of our nation into a beautiful symphony of brotherhood. With this faith we will be able to work together, to pray together, to struggle together, to go to jail together, to stand up for freedom together, knowing that we will be free one day. This will be the day, this will be the day when all of God's children will be able to sing with new meaning:

My country, 'tis of thee, sweet land of liberty, of thee I sing.
Land where my fathers died, land of the pilgrim's pride,
From every mountainside, let freedom ring!

And if America is to be a great nation, this must become true.

And so let freedom ring from the prodigious hilltops of New Hampshire.

Let freedom ring from the mighty mountains of New York.

Let freedom ring from the heightening Alleghenies of Pennsylvania.

Let freedom ring from the snow-capped Rockies of Colorado.

Let freedom ring from the curvaceous slopes of California.

But not only that: Let freedom ring from Stone Mountain of Georgia.

Let freedom ring from Lookout Mountain of Tennessee.

Let freedom ring from every hill and molehill of Mississippi.

From every mountainside, let freedom ring.

And when this happens, when we allow freedom [to] ring, when we let it ring from every village and every hamlet, from every state and every city, we will be able to speed up that day when all of God's children, black men and white men, Jews and Gentiles, Protestants and Catholics, will be able to join hands and sing in the words of the old Negro spiritual:

Free at last! Free at last!

Thank God Almighty, we are free at last!

Reflection Questions

1. Why is Dr. King so insistent that those who are oppressed must resist becoming violent and instead "meet physical force with soul force"? What does this directive suggest about the times and about the people with whom he worked?

2. Discuss the relationship between Dr. King's dream as he set it out here and the American Dream. What are the similarities and differences between the two?

3. Which parts of Dr. King's dream have been realized today and how were they realized? Alternatively, which parts of Dr. King's dream have not yet been realized and what has kept them from being realized?

4. Dr. King used this speech as a rallying cry to end racial discrimination. If this speech were to be updated and given today, what additional groups would be included? Why? What points of his speech remain relevant?

Suffering, Hope,
and the Future

Eulogy for the Martyred Children

On September 15, 1963, Birmingham's Sixteenth Street Baptist Church was bombed, killing eleven-year-old Denise McNair and fourteen-year-old Addie Mae Collins, Carole Robinson, and Cynthia Wesley. Dr. King delivered the following eulogy at a memorial for three of the four victims. The church had been a hub for protests during the spring of 1963 and became a target for the Ku Klux Klan. Dr. King described the murdered children as "martyred heroines of a holy crusade for freedom and dignity" and urged his listeners not to "harbor the desire to retaliate with violence."

This afternoon we gather in the quiet of this sanctuary to pay our last tribute of respect to these beautiful children of God. They entered the stage of history just a few years ago, and in the brief years that they were privileged to act on this mortal stage, they played their parts exceedingly well. Now the curtain falls; they move through the exit; the drama of their earthly life comes to a close. They are now committed back to that eternity from which they came.

These children—unoffending, innocent and beautiful—were the victims of one of the most vicious, heinous crimes ever perpetrated against humanity.

---

*Delivered at the Sixteenth Street Baptist Church,
Birmingham, Alabama, September 18, 1963.*

Yet they died nobly. They are the martyred heroines of a holy crusade for freedom and human dignity. So they have something to say to us in their death. They have something to say to every minister of the gospel who has remained silent behind the safe security of stained-glass windows. They have something to say to every politician who has fed his constituents the stale bread of hatred and the spoiled meat of racism. They have something to say to a federal government that has compromised with the undemocratic practices of southern dixiecrats and the blatant hypocrisy of right-wing northern Republicans. They have something to say to every Negro who passively accepts the evil system of segregation, and stands on the sidelines in the midst of a mighty struggle for justice. They say to each of us, black and white alike, that we must substitute courage for caution. They say to us that we must be concerned not merely about WHO murdered them, but about the system, the way of life and the philosophy which PRODUCED the murderers. Their death says to us that we must work passionately and unrelentingly to make the American dream a reality.

So they did not die in vain. God still has a way of wringing good out of evil. History has proven over and over again that unmerited suffering is redemptive. The innocent blood of these little girls may well serve as the redemptive force that will bring new light to this dark city. The Holy Scripture says, "A little child shall lead them." The death of these little children may lead our whole Southland from the low road of man's inhumanity to man to the high road of peace and brotherhood. These tragic deaths may lead our nation to substitute an aristocracy of character for an aristocracy of color. The spilt blood of these innocent girls may cause the whole citizenry of Birmingham to transform the negative extremes of a dark past into the positive extremes of a bright future. Indeed, this tragic event may cause the white South to come to terms with its conscience.

So in spite of the darkness of this hour we must not despair. We must not become bitter; nor must we harbor the desire to retaliate with violence. We must not lose faith in our white brothers. Somehow we must believe that the most misguided among them can learn to respect the dignity and worth of all human personality.

May I now say a word to you, the members of the bereaved families. It is almost impossible to say anything that can console you at this difficult hour and remove the deep clouds of disappointment which are floating in your mental skies. But I hope you can find a little consolation from the universality of this experience. Death comes to every individual. There is an amazing democracy about death. It is not aristocracy for some of the people, but a democracy for all of the people. Kings die and beggars die; rich men die and poor men die; old people die and young people die; death comes to the innocent and it comes to the guilty. Death is the irreducible common denominator of all men.

I hope you can find some consolation from Christianity's affirmation that death is not the end. Death is not a period that ends the great sentence of life, but a comma that punctuates it to more lofty significance. Death is not a blind alley that leads the human race into a state of nothingness, but an open door which leads man into life eternal. Let this daring faith, this great invincible surmise, be your sustaining power during these trying days.

At times, life is hard, as hard as crucible steel. It has its bleak and painful moments. Like the ever-flowing waters of a river, life has its moments of drought and its moments of flood. Like the ever-changing cycle of the seasons, life has the soothing warmth of the summers and the piercing chill of its winters. But through it all, God walks with us. Never forget that God is able to lift you from fatigue of despair to the buoyancy of hope, and transform dark and desolate valleys into sunlit paths of inner peace.

Your children did not live long, but they lived well. The quantity of their lives was disturbingly small, but the quality of their lives was magnificently big. Where they died and what they were doing when death came will remain a marvelous tribute to each of you and an eternal epitaph to each of them. They died not in a den or dive nor were they hearing and telling filthy jokes at the time of their death. They died within the sacred walls of the church after discussing a principle as eternal as love.

Shakespeare had Horatio utter some beautiful words over the dead body of Hamlet. I paraphrase these words today as I stand over the last remains of these lovely girls.

"Good-night sweet princesses; may the flight of angels take thee to thy eternal rest."

Reflection Questions

1. How does Dr. King use rhetoric to eulogize the young victims? What does he want the audience to understand? Do you think he is successful in his attempts?

2. Dr. King humanizes death in this eulogy. What do you think were the effects of this humanization on the audience, particularly for the families of the victims?

3. In what ways are the young victims potential catalysts for attempts to achieve racial equality?

4. Consider the significance of Dr. King's determination that the victims lived "meaningful lives" despite dying young. What is required to live a meaningful life, in your opinion?

Suffering and Faith

The editor of the *Christian Century* asked Dr. King to write an essay about his intellectual and spiritual development. Prompted to include more about his personal experience in the freedom struggle, Dr. King added the following four paragraphs, which arrived too late to be included in the article when it was published on April 13, 1960.

Some of my personal sufferings over the last few years have also served to shape my thinking. I always hesitate to mention these experiences for fear of conveying the wrong impression. A person who constantly calls attention to his trials and sufferings is in danger of developing a martyr complex and of making others feel that he is consciously seeking sympathy. It is possible for one to be self-centered in his self-denial and self-righteous in his self-sacrifice. So I am always reluctant to refer to my personal sacrifices. But I feel somewhat justified in mentioning them in this article because of the influence they have had in shaping my thinking.

Due to my involvement in the struggle for the freedom of my people, I have known very few quiet days in the last few years. I have been arrested five times and put in Alabama jails. My home has been bombed twice. A day seldom passes that my family and I are not the recipients of threats of death. I have been the victim of a near-fatal stabbing. So in

---

Originally published in the Christian Century *(April 27, 1960).*

a real sense I have been battered by the storms of persecution. I must admit that at times I have felt that I could no longer bear such a heavy burden, and have been tempted to retreat to a more quiet and serene life. But every time such a temptation appeared, something came to strengthen and sustain my determination. I have learned now that the Master's burden is light precisely when we take his yoke upon us.

My personal trials have also taught me the value of unmerited suffering. As my sufferings mounted I soon realized that there were two ways that I could respond to my situation: either to react with bitterness or seek to transform the suffering into a creative force. I decided to follow the latter course. Recognizing the necessity for suffering I have tried to make of it a virtue. If only to save myself from bitterness, I have attempted to see my personal ordeals as an opportunity to transform myself and heal the people involved in the tragic situation which now obtains. I have lived these last few years with the conviction that unearned suffering is redemptive.

There are some who still find the cross a stumbling block, and others consider it foolishness, but I am more convinced than ever before that it is the power of God unto social and individual salvation. So like the Apostle Paul I can now humbly yet proudly say, "I bear in my body the marks of the Lord Jesus." The suffering and agonizing moments through which I have passed over the last few years have also drawn me closer to God. More than ever before I am convinced of the reality of a personal God.

Reflection Questions

1. In your own words, describe Dr. King's belief in the "value of unmerited suffering." What does it mean and what is its purpose?

2. Why would Dr. King be worried about being accused of having a "martyr complex"? Given his explanation in this essay, do you think he *does* or *does not* have a martyr complex?

3. From where does Dr. King draw his strength? Why is that source so important? What does that suggest about his character?

4. Have you ever been tempted to give up on something important to you because the path you were on was difficult, painful, or scary? Where did you draw strength?

The Drum Major Instinct

Dr. King delivered the following sermon—one of his most famous—at Ebenezer Baptist Church on February 4, 1968, just two months before he was assassinated. In the sermon, Dr. King recognizes that many people desire recognition—the "drum major instinct"—but he offers an alternative kind of ambition achieved through a life of service: "I just want to leave a committed life behind."

This morning I would like to use as a subject from which to preach "The Drum Major Instinct." And our text for [this] morning is taken from a very familiar passage in the tenth chapter as recorded by Saint Mark. Beginning with the thirty-fifth verse of that chapter, we read these words: "And James and John, the sons of Zebedee, came unto him saying, 'Master, we would that thou shouldest do for us whatsoever we shall desire.' And he said unto them, 'What would ye that I should do for you?' And they said unto him, 'Grant unto us that we may sit, one on thy right hand, and the other on thy left hand, in thy glory.' But Jesus said unto them, 'Ye know not what ye ask: Can ye drink of the cup that I drink of? and be baptized with the baptism that I am baptized with?' And they said unto him, 'We can.' And Jesus said unto them, 'Ye shall indeed drink of the cup that I drink of, and with the baptism that I am baptized with shall ye be baptized: but to sit on my right hand and

---

Delivered at Ebenezer Baptist Church, Atlanta, Georgia, February 4, 1968.

on my left hand is not mine to give; but it shall be given to them for whom it is prepared.'" And then Jesus goes on toward the end of that passage to say, "But so shall it not be among you: but whosoever will be great among you, shall be your servant: and whosoever of you will be the chiefest, shall be servant of all."

The setting is clear. James and John are making a specific request of the master. They had dreamed, as most of the Hebrews dreamed, of a coming king of Israel who would set Jerusalem free and establish his kingdom on Mount Zion, and in righteousness rule the world. And they thought of Jesus as this kind of king. And they were thinking of that day when Jesus would reign supreme as this new king of Israel. And they were saying, "Now when you establish your kingdom, let one of us sit on the right hand and the other on the left hand of your throne."

Now very quickly, we would automatically condemn James and John, and we would say they were selfish. Why would they make such a selfish request? But before we condemn them too quickly, let us look calmly and honestly at ourselves, and we will discover that we too have those same basic desires for recognition, for importance. That same desire for attention, that same desire to be first. Of course, the other disciples got mad with James and John, and you could understand why, but we must understand that we have some of the same James and John qualities. And there is deep down within all of us an instinct. It's a kind of drum major instinct—a desire to be out front, a desire to lead the parade, a desire to be first. And it is something that runs the whole gamut of life.

And so before we condemn them, let us see that we all have the drum major instinct. We all want to be important, to surpass others, to achieve distinction, to lead the parade. Alfred Adler, the great psychoanalyst, contends that this is the dominant impulse. Sigmund Freud used to contend that sex was the dominant impulse, and Adler came with a new argument saying that this quest for recognition, this desire for attention, this desire for distinction is the basic impulse, the basic drive of human life, this drum major instinct.

And you know, we begin early to ask life to put us first. Our first cry as a baby was a bid for attention. And all through childhood the drum major impulse or instinct is a major obsession. Children ask life to grant them first place. They are a little bundle of ego. And they have innately the drum major impulse or the drum major instinct.

Now, in adult life, we still have it, and we really never get by it. We like to do something good. And you know, we like to be praised for it. Now if you don't believe that, you just go on living life, and you will discover very soon that you like to be praised. Everybody likes it, as a matter of fact. And somehow this warm glow we feel when we are praised or when our name is in print is something of the vitamin A to our ego. Nobody is unhappy when they are praised, even if they know they don't deserve it and even if they don't believe it. The only unhappy people about praise is when that praise is going too much toward somebody else. But everybody likes to be praised because of this real drum major instinct.

Now the presence of the drum major instinct is why so many people are "joiners." You know, there are some people who just join everything. And it's really a quest for attention and recognition and importance. And they get names that give them that impression. So you get your groups, and they become the "Grand Patron," and the little fellow who is henpecked at home needs a chance to be the "Most Worthy of the Most Worthy" of something. It is the drum major impulse and longing that runs the gamut of human life. And so we see it everywhere, this quest for recognition. And we join things, overjoin really, that we think that we will find that recognition in.

Now the presence of this instinct explains why we are so often taken by advertisers. You know, those gentlemen of massive verbal persuasion. And they have a way of saying things to you that kind of gets you into buying. In order to be a man of distinction, you must drink this whiskey. In order to make your neighbors envious, you must drive this type of car. In order to be lovely to love you must wear this kind of lipstick or this kind of perfume. And you know, before you know it, you're just buying that stuff. That's the way the advertisers do it.

I got a letter the other day, and it was a new magazine coming out.

And it opened up, "Dear Dr. King: As you know, you are on many mailing lists. And you are categorized as highly intelligent, progressive, a lover of the arts and the sciences, and I know you will want to read what I have to say." Of course I did. After you said all of that and explained me so exactly, of course I wanted to read it.

But very seriously, it goes through life; the drum major instinct is real. And you know what else it causes to happen? It often causes us to live above our means. It's nothing but the drum major instinct. Do you ever see people buy cars that they can't even begin to buy in terms of their income? You've seen people riding around in Cadillacs and Chryslers who don't earn enough to have a good Model-T Ford. But it feeds a repressed ego.

You know, economists tell us that your automobile should not cost more than half of your annual income. So if you make an income of five thousand dollars, your car shouldn't cost more than about twenty-five hundred. That's just good economics. And if it's a family of two, and both members of the family make ten thousand dollars, they would have to make out with one car. That would be good economics, although it's often inconvenient. But so often, haven't you seen people making five thousand dollars a year and driving a car that costs six thousand? And they wonder why their ends never meet. That's a fact.

Now the economists also say that your house shouldn't cost—if you're buying a house, it shouldn't cost more than twice your income. That's based on the economy and how you would make ends meet. So, if you have an income of five thousand dollars, it's kind of difficult in this society. But say it's a family with an income of ten thousand dollars, the house shouldn't cost much more than twenty thousand. Well, I've seen folk making ten thousand dollars, living in a forty- and fifty-thousand-dollar house. And you know they just barely make it. They get a check every month somewhere, and they owe all of that out before it comes in. Never have anything to put away for rainy days.

But now the problem is, it is the drum major instinct. And you know, you see people over and over again with the drum major instinct taking them over. And they just live their lives trying to outdo the Joneses. They got to get this coat because this particular coat is a little better and a little better-looking than Mary's coat. And I got to drive this car because it's something about this car that makes my car a little better than my neighbor's car. I know a man who used to live in a thirty-five-thousand-dollar house. And other people started building thirty-five-thousand-dollar houses, so he built a seventy-five-thousand-dollar house. And then somebody else built a seventy-five-thousand-dollar house, and he built a hundred-thousand-dollar house. And I don't know where he's going to end up if he's going to live his life trying to keep up with the Joneses.

There comes a time that the drum major instinct can become destructive. And that's where I want to move now. I want to move to the point of saying that if this instinct is not harnessed, it becomes a very dangerous, pernicious instinct. For instance, if it isn't harnessed, it causes one's personality to become distorted. I guess that's the most damaging aspect of it: what it does to the personality. If it isn't harnessed, you will end up day in and day out trying to deal with your ego problem by boasting. Have you ever heard people that—you know, and I'm sure you've met them—that really become sickening because they just sit up all the time talking about themselves? And they just boast and boast and boast, and that's the person who has not harnessed the drum major instinct.

And then it does other things to the personality. It causes you to lie about who you know sometimes. There are some people who are influence peddlers. And in their attempt to deal with the drum major instinct, they have to try to identify with the so-called big-name people. And if you're not careful, they will make you think they know somebody that they don't really know. They know them well, they sip tea with them, and they this-and-that. That happens to people.

And the other thing is that it causes one to engage ultimately in activities that are merely used to get attention. Criminologists tell us that some people are driven to crime because of this drum major instinct. They don't feel that they are getting enough attention through the normal channels of social behavior, and so they turn to anti-social behavior in order to get attention, in order to feel important. And so they get that gun, and before they know it they robbed a bank in a quest for recognition, in a quest for importance.

And then the final great tragedy of the distorted personality is the fact that when one fails to harness this instinct, he ends up trying to push others down in order to push himself up. And whenever you do that, you engage in some of the most vicious activities. You will spread evil, vicious, lying gossip on people, because you are trying to pull them down in order to push yourself up. And the great issue of life is to harness the drum major instinct.

Now the other problem is, when you don't harness the drum major instinct—this uncontrolled aspect of it—is that it leads to snobbish exclusivism. It leads to snobbish exclusivism. And you know, this is the danger of social clubs and fraternities—I'm in a fraternity; I'm in two or three—for sororities and all of these, I'm not talking against them. I'm saying it's the danger. The danger is that they can become forces of classism and exclusivism where somehow you get a degree of satisfaction because you are in something exclusive. And that's fulfilling something, you know—that I'm in this fraternity, and it's the best fraternity in the world, and everybody can't get in this fraternity. So it ends up, you know, a very exclusive kind of thing.

And you know, that can happen with the church; I know churches get in that bind sometimes. I've been to churches, you know, and they say, "We have so many doctors, and so many school teachers, and so many lawyers, and so many businessmen in our church." And that's fine, because doctors need to go to church, and lawyers, and businessmen, teachers—they ought to be in church. But they say that—even the preacher sometimes will go all through that—they say that as if the other people don't count.

And the church is the one place where a doctor ought to forget that he's a doctor. The church is the one place where a PhD ought to forget that he's a PhD. The church is the one place that the school teacher ought to forget the degree she has behind her name. The church is the one place where the lawyer ought to forget that he's a lawyer. And any church that violates the "whosoever will, let him come" doctrine is a dead, cold church, and nothing but a little social club with a thin veneer of religiosity.

When the church is true to its nature, it says, "Whosoever will, let him come." And it [is] not supposed to satisfy the perverted uses of the drum major instinct. It's the one place where everybody should be the same, standing before a common master and savior. And a recognition grows out of this—that all men are brothers because they are children of a common father.

The drum major instinct can lead to exclusivism in one's thinking and can lead one to feel that because he has some training, he's a little better than that person who doesn't have it. Or because he has some economic security, that he's a little better than that person who doesn't have it. And that's the uncontrolled, perverted use of the drum major instinct.

Now the other thing is, that it leads to tragic—and we've seen it happen so often—tragic race prejudice. Many who have written about this problem—Lillian Smith used to say it beautifully in some of her books. And she would say it to the point of getting men and women to see the source of the problem. Do you know that a lot of the race problem grows out of the drum major instinct? A need that some people have to feel superior. A need that some people have to feel that they are first, and to feel that their white skin ordained them to be first. And they have said over and over again in ways that we see with our own eyes. In fact, not too long ago, a man down in Mississippi said that God was a charter member of the White Citizens Council. And so God being the charter member means that everybody who's in that has a kind of divinity, a kind of superiority. And think of what has happened in history as a result of this perverted use of the drum major instinct. It has led to the most tragic prejudice, the most tragic expressions of man's inhumanity to man.

The other day I was saying—I always try to do a little converting when I'm in jail. And when we were in jail in Birmingham the other day, the white wardens and all enjoyed coming around to the cell to talk about the race problem. And they were showing us where we were so wrong demonstrating. And they were showing us where segregation was so right. And they were showing us where intermarriage was so wrong. So I would get to preaching, and we would get to talking—calmly, because they wanted to talk about it. And then we got down one day to the point—that was the second or third day—to talk about where they lived, and how much they were earning. And when those brothers told me what they were earning, I said, "Now, you know what? You ought to be marching with us. You're just as poor as Negroes." And I said, "You are put in the position of supporting your oppressor, because through prejudice and blindness, you fail to see that the same forces that oppress Negroes in American society oppress poor white people. And all you are living on is the satisfaction of your skin being white, and the drum major instinct of thinking that you are somebody big because you are white. And you're so poor you can't send your children to school. You ought to be out here marching with every one of us every time we have a march."

Now that's a fact. That the poor white has been put into this position, where through blindness and prejudice, he is forced to support his oppressors. And the only thing he has going for him is the false feeling that he's superior because his skin is white—and can't hardly eat and make his ends meet week in and week out.

And not only does this thing go into the racial struggle, it goes into the struggle between nations. And I would submit to you this morning that what is wrong in the world today is that the nations of the world are engaged in a bitter, colossal contest for supremacy. And if something doesn't happen to stop this trend, I'm sorely afraid that we won't be here to talk about Jesus Christ and about God and about brotherhood too many more years. If somebody doesn't bring an end to this suicidal thrust that we see in the world today, none of us are going to be around, because somebody's going to make the mistake through our senseless blunderings of dropping a nuclear bomb somewhere. And then another one is going to drop. And don't let anybody fool you, this can happen within a matter of seconds. They have twenty-megaton bombs in Russia right now that can destroy a city as big as New York in three seconds, with everybody wiped away, and every building. And we can do the same thing to Russia and China.

But this is why we are drifting. And we are drifting there because nations are caught up with the drum major instinct. "I must be first." "I must be supreme." "Our nation must rule the world." And I am sad to say that the nation in which we live is the supreme culprit. And I'm going to continue to say it to America, because I love this country too much to see the drift that it has taken.

God didn't call America to do what she's doing in the world now. God didn't call America to engage in a senseless, unjust war as the war in Vietnam. And we are criminals in that war. We've committed more war crimes almost than any nation in the world, and I'm going to continue to say it. And we won't stop it because of our pride and our arrogance as a nation.

But God has a way of even putting nations in their place. The God that I worship has a way of saying, "Don't play with me." He has a way of saying, as the God of the Old Testament used to say to the Hebrews, "Don't play with me, Israel. Don't play with me, Babylon. Be still and know that I'm God. And if you don't stop your reckless course, I'll rise up and break the backbone of your power." And that can happen to America. Every now and then I go back and read Gibbons' *Decline and Fall of the Roman Empire*. And when I come and look at America, I say to myself, "The parallels are frightening. And we have perverted the drum major instinct."

A TIME TO BREAK SILENCE

But let me rush on to my conclusion, because I want you to see what Jesus was really saying. What was the answer that Jesus gave these men? It's very interesting. One would have thought that Jesus would have condemned them. One would have thought that Jesus would have said, "You are out of your place. You are selfish. Why would you raise such a question?"

But that isn't what Jesus did; he did something altogether different. He said in substance, "Oh, I see, you want to be first. You want to be great. You want to be important. You want to be significant. Well, you ought to be. If you're going to be my disciple, you must be." But he reordered priorities. And he said, "Yes, don't give up this instinct. It's a good instinct if you use it right. It's a good instinct if you don't distort it and pervert it. Don't give it up. Keep feeling the need for being important. Keep feeling the need for being first. But I want you to be first in love. I want you to be first in moral excellence. I want you to be first in generosity. That is what I want you to do."

And he transformed the situation by giving a new definition of greatness. And you know how he said it? He said, "Now brethren, I can't give you greatness. And really, I can't make you first." This is what Jesus said to James and John. "You must earn it. True greatness comes not by favoritism, but by fitness. And the right hand and the left are not mine to give, they belong to those who are prepared."

And so Jesus gave us a new norm of greatness. If you want to be important—wonderful. If you want to be recognized—wonderful. If you want to be great—wonderful. But recognize that he who is greatest among you shall be your servant. That's a new definition of greatness.

And this morning, the thing that I like about it: By giving that definition of greatness, it means that everybody can be great, because everybody can serve. You don't have to have a college degree to serve. You don't have to make your subject and your verb agree to serve. You don't have to know about Plato and Aristotle to serve. You don't have to know Einstein's theory of relativity to serve. You don't have to know the second theory of thermodynamics in physics to serve. You only need a heart full of grace, a soul generated by love. And you can be that servant.

I know a man—and I just want to talk about him a minute, and maybe you will discover who I'm talking about as I go down the way because he was a great one. And he just went about serving. He was born in an obscure village, the child of a poor peasant woman. And then he grew up in still another obscure village, where he worked as a carpenter until he was thirty years old. Then for three years, he just got on his feet, and he was an itinerant preacher. And he went about doing some things. He didn't have much. He never wrote a book. He never held an office. He never had a family. He never owned a house. He never went to college. He never visited a big city. He never went two hundred miles from where he was born. He did none of the usual things that the world would associate with greatness. He had no credentials but himself.

He was only thirty-three when the tide of public opinion turned against him. They called him a rabble-rouser. They called him a trouble-maker. They said he was an agitator. He practiced civil disobedience; he broke injunctions. And so he was turned over to his enemies and went through the mockery of a trial. And the irony of it all is that his friends turned him over to them. One of his closest friends denied him. Another of his friends turned him over to his enemies. And while he was dying, the people who killed him gambled for his clothing, the only possession that he had in the world. When he was dead he was buried in a borrowed tomb, through the pity of a friend.

Nineteen centuries have come and gone and today he stands as the most influential figure that ever entered human history. All of the armies that ever marched, all the navies that ever sailed, all the parliaments that ever sat, and all the kings that ever reigned put together have not affected the life of man on this earth as much as that one solitary life. His name may be a familiar one. But today I can hear them talking about him. Every now and then somebody says, "He's King of Kings." And again I can hear somebody saying, "He's Lord of Lords." Somewhere else

I can hear somebody saying, "In Christ there is no East nor West." And then they go on and talk about, "In Him there's no North and South, but one great Fellowship of Love throughout the whole wide world." He didn't have anything. He just went around serving and doing good.

This morning, you can be on his right hand and his left hand if you serve. It's the only way in.

Every now and then I guess we all think realistically about that day when we will be victimized with what is life's final common denominator—that something that we call death. We all think about it. And every now and then I think about my own death and I think about my own funeral. And I don't think of it in a morbid sense. And every now and then I ask myself, "What is it that I would want said?" And I leave the word to you this morning.

If any of you are around when I have to meet my day, I don't want a long funeral. And if you get somebody to deliver the eulogy, tell them not to talk too long. And every now and then I wonder what I want them to say. Tell them not to mention that I have a Nobel Peace Prize— that isn't important. Tell them not to mention that I have three or four hundred other awards—that's not important. Tell them not to mention where I went to school.

I'd like somebody to mention that day that Martin Luther King, Jr., tried to give his life serving others.

I'd like for somebody to say that day that Martin Luther King, Jr., tried to love somebody.

I want you to say that day that I tried to be right on the war question.

I want you to be able to say that day that I did try to feed the hungry.

And I want you to be able to say that day that I did try in my life to clothe those who were naked.

I want you to say on that day that I did try in my life to visit those who were in prison.

I want you to say that I tried to love and serve humanity.

Yes, if you want to say that I was a drum major, say that I was a drum major for justice. Say that I was a drum major for peace. I was a drum major for righteousness. And all of the other shallow things will not matter. I won't have any money to leave behind. I won't have the fine and luxurious things of life to leave behind. But I just want to leave a committed life behind. And that's all I want to say.

> If I can help somebody as I pass along,
> If I can cheer somebody with a word or song,
> If I can show somebody he's traveling wrong,
> Then my living will not be in vain.
> If I can do my duty as a Christian ought,
> If I can bring salvation to a world once wrought,
> If I can spread the message as the master taught,
> Then my living will not be in vain.

Yes, Jesus, I want to be on your right or your left side, not for any selfish reason. I want to be on your right or your left side, not in terms of some political kingdom or ambition. But I just want to be there in love and in justice and in truth and in commitment to others, so that we can make of this old world a new world.

Reflection Questions

1. What is the drum major instinct? Describe it in your own words.

2. Why is the drum major instinct unfavorable? In what ways is the drum major instinct destructive?

3. How does the drum major instinct allow the perpetuation of discrimination?

4. What suggestions does Dr. King offer about preventing the drum major instinct in his directions for how he wants to be eulogized? What do these suggestions imply about his understanding of the importance and the legacy of his work?

What Is Your Life's Blueprint?

On October 26, 1967, six months before he was assassinated, Dr. King spoke to a group of students at Barratt Junior High School in Philadelphia, Pennsylvania. As in many of his other speeches, King invokes the street sweeper as a lowly occupation and then elevates it as a model for how to be the best one can be, regardless of one's status in life.

I want to ask you a question, and that is, What is in your life's blueprint? This is a most important and crucial period of your lives, for what you do now and what you decide now at this age may well determine which way your life shall go. And whenever a building is constructed, you usually have an architect who draws a blueprint. And that blueprint serves as the pattern, as the guide, as the model for those who are to build the building. And a building is not well erected without a good, sound, and solid blueprint.

Now, each of you is in the process of building the structure of your lives. And the question is whether you have a proper, a solid, and a sound blueprint. And I want to suggest some of the things that should be in your life's blueprint.

Number one in your life's blueprint should be a deep belief in your own dignity, your own worth, and your own somebodiness. Don't

---

Delivered at Barratt Junior High School, Philadelphia,
Pennsylvania, October 26, 1967.

allow anybody to make you feel that you are nobody. Always feel that you count. Always feel that you have worth. And always feel that your life has ultimate significance. Now, that means that you should not be ashamed of your color. You know, it's very unfortunate that in so many instances, our society has placed a stigma on the Negroes' color. And you know there are some Negroes who are ashamed of themselves. But don't be ashamed of your color. Don't be ashamed of your biological features. Somehow you must be able to say in your own lives—and really believe it—"I am black but beautiful," and believe it in your heart. And therefore you need not be lured into purchasing cosmetics advertised to make you lighter. Neither do you need to process your hair to make it appear straight. I have good hair, and it is good as anybody else's hair in the world, and we've got to believe that.

Now, in your life's blueprint, be sure that you have that principle of somebodiness. Secondly, in your life's blueprint, you must have as a basic principle the determination to achieve excellence in your various fields of endeavor. You're going to be deciding, as the days and the years unfold, what you will do in life, what your life's work will be. And once you discover what it will be, set out to do it, and to do it well. And I say to you, my young friends, that doors are opening to each of you, doors of opportunity are opening to each of you that were not open to your mothers and to your fathers. And the great challenge facing you is to be ready to enter these doors as they open.

Ralph Waldo Emerson, the great essayist, said in a lecture back in 1871 that if a man can write a better book or preach a better sermon or make a better mousetrap than his neighbor, even if he builds his house in the woods, the world will make a beaten path to his door. That hadn't always been true, but it will become increasingly true. And so I would urge you to study hard, to burn the midnight oil. I would say to you, "Don't drop out of school." And I understand all of the sociological reasons why we often drop out of school. But I urge you, in spite of your economic plight, in spite of the situation that you are forced to live so often with intolerable conditions, stay in school.

And when you discover what you're going to be in life, set out to do it as if God Almighty called you at this particular moment in history to do it. And just don't set out to do a good Negro job, but do a good job that anybody could do. Don't set out to be just a good Negro doctor, a good Negro lawyer, a good Negro schoolteacher, a good Negro preacher, a good Negro barber or beautician, a good Negro skilled laborer. For if you set out to do that, you have already flunked your matriculation exam for entrance into the University of Integration. Set out to do a good job, and do that job so well that the living, the dead, or the unborn couldn't do it any better.

If it falls to your lot to be a street sweeper, sweep streets like Michelangelo painted pictures. Sweep streets like Beethoven composed music. Sweep streets like Leontyne Price sings before the Metropolitan Opera. And sweep streets like Shakespeare wrote poetry. Sweep streets so well that all the hosts of Heaven and Earth will have to pause and say, "Here lived a great street sweeper who swept his job well."

If you can't be a pine on the top of the hill, be a scrub in the valley. But be the best little scrub on the side of the hill. Be a bush if you can't be a tree. If you can't be a highway, just be a trail. If you can't be the sun, be a star. For it isn't by size that you win or you fail. Be the best of whatever you are.

We already have some noble examples of black men and black women who demonstrated to us that human nature cannot be catalogued. They and their own lives have walked through long and desolate nights of oppression, and yet they've risen up and plunged against cloud-filled nights of affliction. New and blazing stars of inspiration.

And, so, from an old slaves' cabin of Virginia's hills, Booker T. Washington rose up to be one of America's great leaders. He lit a torch in Alabama, and darkness fled in that setting. Yes, you should know this because it's in your own city.

From a poverty-stricken area of Philadelphia, Pennsylvania, Marian Anderson rose up to be the world's greatest contralto, so that a Toscanini could say that a voice like this comes only once in a century, and Sibelius of Finland could say, "My roof is too low for such a voice."

From the red hills of Gordon County, Georgia, in the arms of a mother who could neither read nor write, Roland Hayes rose up to be one of the world's great singers and carried his melodious voice into the palaces and mansions of kings and queens.

From crippling circumstances there came a George Washington Carver to carve for himself an imperishable niche in the annals of science.

There was a star in the diplomatic sky. And then came Ralph Bunche, the grandson of a slave preacher, and he reached up and grabbed it and allowed it to shine in his life with all of its scintillating beauty. There was a star in the athletic sky, and then came Jackie Robinson in his day and Willie Mays in his day, with their powerful bats and their calm spirits. Then came Jesse Owens, with his fleeting, dashing feet. Then came Joe Louis and Muhammad Ali, with their educated fists. All of them came to tell us that we can be somebody. And to justify the conviction of the poet:

> *Fleecy locks and black complexion*
> *Cannot forfeit nature's claim;*
> *Skins may differ, but affection*
> *Dwells in white and black the same.*

> *And if I were so tall as to reach the pole*
> *Or to grasp at the ocean at a span,*
> *I must be measured by my soul*
> *The mind is the standard of the man.**

And finally, and finally, in your life's blueprint, must be a commitment to the eternal principles of beauty, love, and justice. Don't allow

---

*The first part of the poem Dr. King reads is from William Cowper's "The Negro's Complaint" (1788); the second is from Isaac Watts's "False Greatness" (1706), from *Horae Lyricae*, book II.

anybody to pull you so low as to make you hate them. Don't allow anybody to cause you to lose your self-respect to the point that you do not struggle for justice. However young you are, you have a responsibility to seek to make your nation a better nation in which to live. You have a responsibility to seek to make life better for everybody. And so you must be involved in the struggle for freedom and justice.

Now, in this struggle for freedom and justice, there are many constructive things that we all can do and that we all must do. And we must not give ourselves to those things which will not solve our problems. You've heard the word "nonviolent" and you've heard the word "violent." I happen to believe in nonviolence. We struggle with this method with young people and adults alike, all over the South, and we have won some significant victories. And we've got to struggle with it all over the North, because the problems are as serious in the North as they are in the South.

But I believe as we struggle with these problems, we've got to struggle with them with a method that can be militant but at the same time does not destroy life or property. And so our slogan must not be "Burn, baby, burn." It must be, "Build, baby, build." "Organize, baby, organize." Yes, our slogan must be "Learn, baby, learn," so that we can earn, baby, earn.

And with a powerful commitment, I believe that we can transform dark yesterdays of injustice into bright tomorrows of justice and humanity. Let us keep going toward the goal of selfhood, toward the realization of the dream of brotherhood, and toward the realization of the dream of understanding good will. Let nobody stop us.

I close by quoting once more the man that the young lady quoted, that magnificent black bard who has now passed on, Langston Hughes. One day he wrote a poem entitled "Mother to Son." The mother didn't always have her grammar right, but she uttered words of great symbolic profundity:

> *Well, son, I'll tell you:*
> *Life for me ain't been no crystal stair.*

It's had tacks in it,
[And splinters,]
And boards torn up,
places with no carpet on the floor—
Bare.
But all the time
I'se been a-climbin' on,
And reachin' landin's,
And turnin' corners,
And sometimes goin' in the dark
Where there ain't been no light.
So boy, don't you stop now.
Don't you set down on the steps
'Cause you finds it's kinder hard.
For I'se still goin', boy,
I'se still climbin',
And life for me ain't been no crystal stair.

Well, life for none of us has been a crystal stair. But we must keep moving. We must keep going. If you can't fly, run. If you can't run, walk. If you can't walk, crawl. But by all means, keep moving.

Reflection Questions

1. What does Dr. King mean by "somebodiness"? What does it suggest about Dr. King's opinion of young people that he has taken a break from a packed schedule to talk to a group of students? Further, what does it suggest about his belief in young people when he tells them they "have a responsibility to seek to make your nation a better nation in which to live"?

2. What is the importance of the message that anyone can be the best at something if he or she pursues excellence?

3. How does Dr. King offer inspiration in this essay? How does he provide advice about how to silence naysayers?

4. What is in *your* life's blueprint? What do you think is required to make that blueprint a reality?

Acknowledgments

Beacon Press gratefully acknowledges the King Legacy for Students' teacher advisory board, including Ken Chiusano, Vaughan O. Danvers, James Morris, Rohini A. Parikh, and Rachel Tsivitis. Special thanks are given to Dr. Kimberly N. Parker, editorial advisor, and Andrea McEvoy Spero, curriculum advisor to the King Legacy for Students.

Beacon Press also expresses heartfelt gratitude to the Estate of Dr. Martin Luther King, Jr., Dr. Clayborne Carson and the Martin Luther King, Jr. Research and Education Institute at Stanford University, Michele Rubin, Geri Thoma, Amy Berkower, Simon Lipskar, Brianne Johnson, Writers House, Walter Dean Myers, Miriam Altshuler, and the Philadelphia School District.

Publication of the King Legacy Series would not be possible without the generous support of the Unitarian Universalist Veatch Program at Shelter Rock.

Glossary

Abernathy, Ralph (1926–1990). Baptist preacher. Joined Dr. King to organize a boycott of the Birmingham, Alabama, bus system; also founded the Southern Christian Leadership Conference (SCLC) with Dr. King.

agape. One of the four Ancient Greek words for love; *agape* means selfless, sacrificial, unconditional love, the highest of the four types of love in the Bible; other types of love include *eros* (romantic), *storge* (familial), and *philia* (friendship).

Alabama Christian Movement for Human Rights (ACMHR). An organization founded in Birmingham, Alabama, on June 5, 1956, after the NAACP was banned in the state; shared similar integration goals and joined the Southern Christian Leadership Conference in 1957.

anarchy. The absence of government.

Azikiwe, Nnamdi (1904–1996). First president of independent Nigeria; governed from 1963 to 1966.

Banda, Hastings Kamuzu (1898–1997). First president of Malawi and primary leader of the Malawi Nationalist movement; governed Malawi from 1963 to 1994.

Bevel, James (1936–2008). An advisor to Dr. King; persuaded Dr. King to involve young people in the Children's Crusade in 1963 in Birmingham, Alabama.

Bhoodan Movement. Also known as the Land-Gift Movement; started by Vinoba Bhave, a follower of Mahatma Gandhi; gave land to those without and to the poor through voluntary donations of land.

bigotry. Hostility toward members of a group based on members' beliefs, behaviors, or appearance.

Billups, Charles (1927?–1968). A founder of the Alabama Christian Movement for Human Rights in 1954; a founder of Operation Breadbasket in Chicago, an economic arm of the Southern Christian Leadership Conference (SCLC).

boycott. A refusal to buy or use products or services in order to convince businesses or organizations to change practices seen as unjust.

Buddhism. Founded by Siddhartha Gautama, practitioners follow the Four Noble Truths: the truth of suffering, the truth of the cause of suffering, the truth of the end of suffering, and that the true path leads to the end of suffering; also advocates karma and the cycle of rebirth.

Bunche, Ralph J. (1904–1971). The first African American to be awarded a Nobel Peace Prize (1950) for his mediation with Palestine as part of a United Nations mission; was also a scholar-activist and promoted the intellectual needs of African American students.

capitalism. An economic system characterized by private ownership, limited government involvement, and the ability to privately control prices of goods and services; the primary goal is to make a profit for owners and shareholders; can result in monopolies of power and unequal distribution of wealth.

caste system. A social structure that defines and categorizes people based on social status within a hierarchy.

civil contempt. A failure to follow a court order that benefits someone else.

civil disobedience. Public, nonviolent action intended to change laws and policies.

classism. Prejudice or discrimination based on social class.

colonialism. Governance of a nation or group of people by another nation; the controlling nation imposes its own policies and procedures upon the governed, usually with little regard for indigenous customs.

Communism. A system of shared ownership of property within a community. During much of the twentieth century, Communism was associated with the Soviet Union and was seen as a threat to democracy and to the United States.

Connor, T. Eugene "Bull" (1897–1973). Birmingham, Alabama, commissioner of public safety and vocal segregationist; gave the order to turn water hoses and unleash police dogs on peaceful protestors.

Cotton, Dorothy (1930–). Director of the Southern Christian Leadership Conference (SCLC) Citizen Education Program (CEP); the highest-ranking woman in the SCLC for most of the 1960s; member of Dr. King's executive committee.

criminal contempt. Conduct that displays disrespect for or interference with the legal process (for example, disobeying a court order can land one in contempt).

degradation. The process of demeaning with the goal of reducing the status of a person or group.

dictator. A person granted complete authority or power, generally over a country.

dissent. To disagree with an idea or opinion; a disagreement.

Dixiecrats. Also called States Rights' Democrats; right-wing splinter group started in 1948 by Southerners who objected to the civil rights program of the Democratic Party; nominated Strom Thurmond of South Carolina for the 1948 presidential election.

doctrine. A set of guidelines and principles that are taught or articulated to others.

Du Bois, W. E. B. (1868–1963). Cofounder of the National Association for the Advancement of Colored People (NAACP); first African American to earn a doctorate from Harvard; author of *The Souls of Black Folk*, a collection of fourteen essays; clashed with Booker T. Washington over racial ideologies.

ecclesiastical. Of or related to a church; suitable for use in a church.

emancipation. Freedom from bondage or slavery.

Emancipation Proclamation. Issued by President Abraham Lincoln on January 1, 1863; granted freedom to slaves in states not under Union control; also allowed black soldiers to fight for the Union side in the Civil War.

eros. One of the four Ancient Greek words for love, *eros* is the intimate or romantic love shared between two people. Other types of love include *storge* (familial), *philia* (friendship), and *agape* (unconditional).

ethical relativism. The belief that nothing is simply right or wrong but that the perception of right or wrong depends on the individual, culture, or historical period.

extremist. A person who goes to extremes, especially in political matters.

Franklin, C. L. (1915–1984). Called the Pastor of Millions for selling millions of copies of his seventy-six recorded sermons; organizer of the Detroit Freedom March in June 1963, which drew Dr. King and more than 500,000 people, and where Dr. King delivered an early version of his "I Have a Dream" speech.

Freedom Ride Movement. A series of political protests against seg-regation in which blacks and whites rode buses together through the American South in 1961.

Gandhi, Mohandas K. (1869–1948). Indian leader who used nonviolent resistance to champion the rights of all Indians; leader of India's inde-pendence movement and responsible for inspiring many internationally to consider nonviolence.

Garvey, Marcus (1887–1940). Jamaican social activist who endorsed the Nationalism and Pan-Africanism movements; founded the Universal Negro Improvement Association (UNIA) and African Communities League; creator of the "Back to Africa" movement.

Geneva Agreement. Settlements from the 1954 Geneva Conference that ended the Vietnam War.

GI Bill of Rights. Officially called the Serviceman's Readjustment Act of 1944; allows servicemen and -women returning from war to resume their education upon discharge; also provides home loans, unemploy-ment wages, and other provisions.

Goethe, Johann Wolfgang von (1749–1832). Considered the greatest German literary figure of the modern era; poet, playwright, novelist, scientist, statesman, theatre director, critic, and amateur artist.

gradualism. The process of attaining a result through gradual means.

guerrilla. A member of an independent group intent on subverting au-thority through sabotage, war, or other types of unsanctioned conflict.

ideology. A system of thought or set of theories about human culture and society.

imperialism. A nation's process of taking over another country or terri-tory, either through direct or indirect governance.

indignity. Offensive actions against someone's self-esteem.

integration. The combination of people of different groups (usually races) into an organization or institution.

Jemison, Theodore (1919–). Leader of a bus boycott in Baton Rouge, Louisiana, in 1953 that was a model for the Montgomery bus boycott; one of the founding members of the Southern Christian Leadership Conference (SCLC).

Jim Crow. Refers to a system of laws that legalized segregation in the United States; the term originated with a popular nineteenth-century minstrel song that stereotyped African Americans.

jumboism. Approval or respect for objects or ideas based on their large size.

Ku Klux Klan (KKK). Founded in 1866; white hate group that perpetrated violence and intimidation against any person or organization that differed with its views, primarily African Americans, Jews, and Catholics.

Lee, Bernard (1935–1991). Student leader of the Alabama sit-in movement; Dr. King's personal assistant throughout the 1960s.

Little Rock Nine. The group of nine students barred from matriculating at Little Rock High School in Arkansas in 1957 until an executive order by President Dwight Eisenhower forced their admittance. The students were Minnijean Brown, Elizabeth Eckford, Ernest Green, Thelma Mothershed, Melba Pattillo, Gloria Ray, Terrence Roberts, Jefferson Thomas, and Carlotta Walls.

Lumumba, Patrice (1925–1961). First prime minister of the Democratic Republic of the Congo; forced out of political office during a political crisis and assassinated soon thereafter.

lynching. Intimidation, terrorism, and murder of blacks by mobs of whites; often performative or social events for whites; most were hangings or shootings.

Marshall, Burke (1922–2003). Head of the US Justice Department's Civil Rights Division under Presidents Kennedy and Johnson; Dr. King regularly contacted Marshall for assistance.

martyrdom. Suffering or dying because of loyalty to an idea, belief, or one's religious beliefs.

Marxism. The political, economic, and social principles advocated by Karl Marx; a theory and practice of socialism including the labor theory of value, dialectical materialism, the class struggle, and a dictatorship of the proletariat until the establishment of a classless society.

Mboya, Thomas (1930–1969). Kenyan politician; formed People's Convention Party; assassinated six years after Kenya gained independence.

metaphysical materialism. The theory that a world would still exist even if one did not believe it existed.

Minh, Ho Chi (1890–1969). Leader of the Vietnamese National Movement for more than three decades; president of North Vietnam from 1954 until his death.

Montgomery Advertiser. Daily newspaper of Montgomery, Alabama; founded in 1829.

Montgomery Improvement Association (MIA). Formed on December 5, 1955, by black ministers and community leaders in Montgomery, Alabama; led by Dr. King and instrumental in guiding the Montgomery bus boycott.

National Association for the Advancement of Colored People (NAACP). Founded on February 12, 1909, by a group of whites and blacks to address lynching and race riots; nation's oldest, largest, and most widely recognized grassroots-based civil rights organization.

nationalist. An individual or political party promoting a centralized national government.

Nation of Islam. Black Nationalist organization founded in Detroit in 1930 by Wallace D. Fard; promoted improvement of African American lives; accused of being racist and anti-Semitic.

Nietzsche, Friedrich (1844–1900). German philosopher of the late nineteenth century who challenged the foundations of Christianity and traditional morality.

Nixon, Edgar Daniel "E. D." (1899–1987). Head of the Montgomery, Alabama, branch of the Pullman Porters union and president of the local NAACP; bailed Rosa Parks out of jail; one of the primary organizers of the Montgomery bus boycott and the Montgomery Improvement Association.

Nkrumah, Kwame (1909–1972). Ghanaian leader important for securing Ghana's independence from Britain; president for life until forced out of power in 1966.

oppression. Unjust or cruel exercise of authority or power.

Ovid. Ancient Roman poet famous for writing *Metamorphoses*, a rich source of Greek and Roman mythology.

philia. An Ancient Greek term for love, this is the type of love shared between friends; other types of love include *storge* (familial), *eros* (romantic), and *agape* (unconditional).

Plato (429–347 BCE). One of the most influential philosophers and instrumental in the development of philosophy.

propaganda. Information that is manipulated for the purpose of promoting or damaging a group, person, or idea.

Raj Ghat. A memorial to Mahatma Gandhi held in Delhi, India, every Friday, the day of his death.

Reconstruction (1865–1877). Post–Civil War attempt to address the needs of newly freed African American populations; initiatives included voting, land ownership, and education; resulted in Black Codes and other forms of white supremacy as protest.

Reddick, Lawrence (1910–1995). Historian and biographer of Dr. King (*Crusader Without Violence*); appointed by Dr. King as chairman of the Montgomery Improvement Association's History Committee to record events of the Montgomery bus boycott.

segregation. The intentional separation of a race, class, or ethnic group from others through discrimination in housing, schools, businesses, or other institutions.

Senior Citizens Committee. Business-leadership organization in Birmingham, Alabama, that was responsible for negotiating in 1963 with the Southern Christian Leadership Council to end protests by African Americans and begin the process of desegregation.

Shuttlesworth, Fred (1922–2011). A founder of the Alabama Christian Movement for Human Rights (ACMHR) and of the Southern Christian Leadership Conference (SCLC); key proponent for local efforts for black equality in Alabama; responsible for bringing Dr. King to Birmingham, Alabama, in 1963 for desegregation efforts.

Smith, Lillian (1897–1966). White Southern author who used her writing to criticize racism; best known for *Strange Fruit* (1944) and *Killers of the Dream* (1949), which challenged ideas about interracial relationships and racial segregation.

Southern Christian Leadership Conference (SCLC). Umbrella association established in 1957 to coordinate local protests throughout the South after the success of the Montgomery bus boycott under Dr. King's leadership.

status quo. An unchanged condition.

theological. Having to do with God, the study of God, or religion.

tokenism. Resistance to actual desegregation through a figurative attempt, rather than a genuine attempt.

totalitarianism. Consolidated control by a tyrannical authority.

untouchables/*dalits*. In India, those comprising the lowest social caste in the Hindu caste system; over 167 million in population, they face discrimination on many levels, including access to education and medical care, as well as where they are allowed to live, sit, and eat.

Walker, Wyatt Tee (1929–). Appointed Dr. King's chief of staff in 1960 and served as first full-time executive director of the Southern Christian Leadership Council; known for his financial and organizational acumen.

Washington, Booker T. (1856–1915). Founded the Tuskegee Institute in Alabama; focused on training African Americans in agricultural pursuits; clashed with W. E. B. Du Bois over racial ideologies.

White Citizens Council (WCC). Middle- and upper-class white segregationists who used violence and intimidation; relied on social and economic tactics.

Wright, Richard (1908–1960). African American journalist, author, and poet; famous for his books *Black Boy* and *Native Son*.

Young, Andrew (1932–). Organized Citizenship Schools for the Southern Christian Leadership Conference and Dr. King; eventually became executive director; instrumental in organizing voter registration and desegregation campaigns throughout the South; was with Dr. King when he was assassinated.

Index

THE KING LEGACY SERIES

In partnership with the Estate of Dr. Martin Luther King, Jr., Beacon Press is proud to share the great privilege and responsibility of furthering Dr. King's powerful message of peace, nonviolence, and social justice with a historic publishing program—the King Legacy.

The series encompasses Dr. King's most important writings, including sermons, orations, lectures, prayers, and all of his previously published books that are currently out of print. Published accessibly and in multiple formats, each volume includes new material from acclaimed scholars and activists, underscoring Dr. King's continued relevance for the twenty-first century and bringing his message to a new generation of readers.

Clayborne Carson is general editorial advisor to the King Legacy and is director of the Martin Luther King, Jr. Research and Education Institute at Stanford University.

thekinglegacy.org

Library of Congress Cataloging-in-Publication Data

King, Martin Luther, Jr., 1929–1968.
[Works. Selections]
A time to break silence : the essential works of Martin Luther King, Jr. for students /
Martin Luther King, Jr. ; introduction by Walter Dean Myers.
pages cm. — (King Legacy series)
"Published under the auspices of the Unitarian Universalist Association of Congregations."
Includes bibliographical references and index.
ISBN 978-0-8070-3318-0 (cloth : alk. paper) — ISBN 978-0-8070-3305-0 (pbk. : alk. paper) —
ISBN 978-0-8070-3306-7 (ebook)
1. African Americans—Civil rights. 2. Civil rights movements—United States—History—
20th century. 3. Nonviolence. I. Myers, Walter Dean, 1937– editor of compilation. II. Title.
E185.97.K5A25 2013   323.092—dc23
2013012953